Welcome to

Shaping Hearts with God's Word

Thank you for choosing HeartShaper Children's Curriculum. With HeartShaper curriculum, you'll find resources designed to help you . . .

REACH kids with special needs

a quarterly newsletter that teachers can use for adapting lessons and including children who have special needs.
- General tips and encouragement for teachers
- Age-specific ways to adapt activities included in HeartShaper lessons
- Ideas for helping families of children with special needs

LEAD kids to Christ

a pocket guide designed to help teachers and volunteers lead a child to a personal relationship with Jesus.
- Quick reference for teachers including tips for where to start and what to ask kids
- Scripture references to help a child learn what it means to have a personal relationship with Jesus
- Ideas to guide children through God's Word and provide ongoing encouragement

CONNECT with HeartShaper community

a resourceful website including discussion forums with topics relevant to children's ministry leaders, teachers, and volunteers.
Ask questions, share ideas, and get connected!

TRAIN yourself and your team

online resources including free downloads, recruiting and training videos, PowerPoint presentations, and more!
Feel confident teaching HeartShaper lessons right from the start!

Learn more at www.heartshaper.com

How to Use **HeartShaper**®

- Read the introductory pages and the unit pages.
- Use the correlated HeartShaper materials.
- Pray for God's help to guide children to a personal relationship with Jesus Christ.

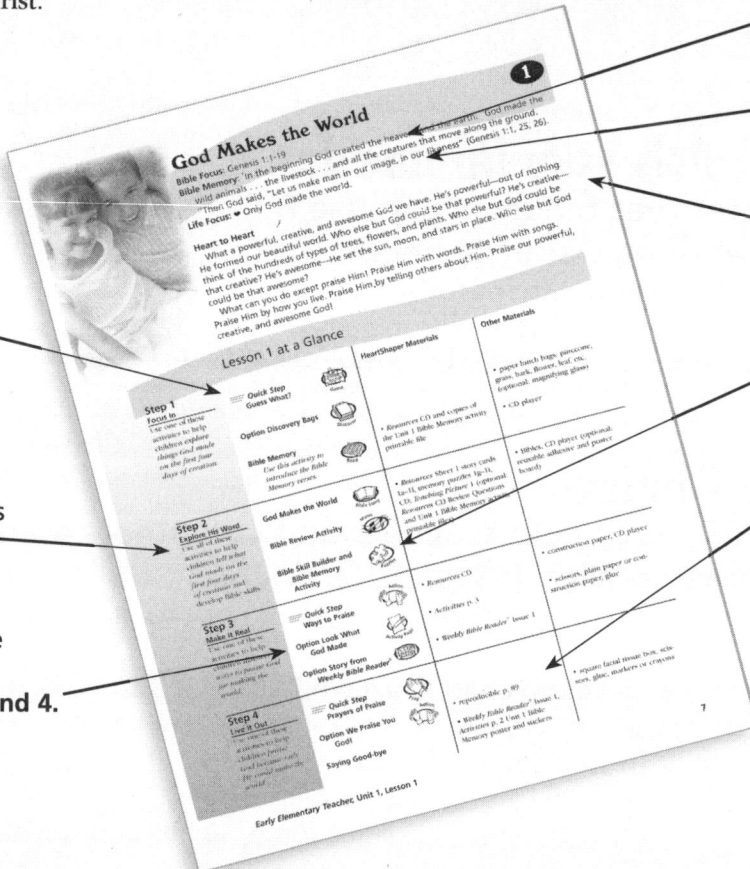

Bible Memory for children to learn.

Life Focus is the main thought children will learn and remember.

Heart to Heart provides inspirational thoughts for teachers.

Quick Step activities are easy to prepare.

Use all the activities in **Step 2**.

Optional activities are included in **Steps 1, 3, and 4.**

Activity icons identify at a glance the types of activities offered.

Materials included in HeartShaper curriculum.

Special Note
If you are part of a rotating team of teachers, meet together to pray and plan. Work together on developing a basic schedule for class sessions, establishing class rules and consequences, planning service projects and parties, and decorating the room.

Step 1 Focus In: Children explore the lesson theme and are introduced to the Bible Memory.

Step 2 Explore His Word: Children explore what the Bible says, learn Bible skills, and learn Bible Memory verses.

Step 3 Make It Real: Children discover how the lessons learned from the Bible relate to their lives.

Step 4 Live It Out: Children either *do* what has been learned or plan *how* to do it.

You can adapt this curriculum!

- ❤ Use this curriculum with a large group/small group format. You could do Steps 1, 3, and 4 in small groups and Step 2 in a large group.
- ❤ Use this curriculum with a team approach. Have different team members plan and lead activities in each of the steps.
- ❤ For additional learning activities, use more than one activity option per step.
- ❤ Use unused options for a weekday program.

Have a Plan

Online Helps
- A modifiable newsletter is available online to help you connect with families of children in your class.
- Look for seasonal and holiday ideas to help children remember God and celebrate Jesus all year long.
- Apply the online training tips to your teaching and grow in your effectiveness to reach today's kids with God's Word.

Go to www.heartshaper.com.

HeartShaper E-news
Sign up to receive a weekly newsletter with expert tips and free downloads you can use in the classroom. Go to www.heartshaper.com.

Shaping
hearts
with
God's
Word

● **Plan ahead.**
Prepare your room with basic supplies, age-appropriate furniture, and interesting things to look at. Do you need an offering container, *New International Version* classroom Bibles, additional activity books, a CD player, or a first-aid kit? Plan to be in class before the first child arrives.

● **Plan for classroom management.**
Before class, give enough time to preparation. Understand the characteristics of early elementary children and teach accordingly. Pray for yourself and the children you teach. During class, show the children that you care about them. Know their names and use them. Never raise your voice. Post rules and make sure children understand why certain behaviors are unacceptable. Always expect good behavior.

● **Plan to be safe.**
Know your church's security guidelines and follow them. You should have guidelines about dismissing children, teacher-to-child ratios, and restroom breaks. Know the location of first-aid supplies. Before you serve snacks, be aware of any allergies children may have. Make sure you have plans for what to do when a fire alarm sounds or in the case of severe weather. Know where each child's parents or guardians are during the time children are in class.

● **Plan to include all children.**
Some of the children in your class will be from single-parent homes, blended families, and/or foster homes. Some children may have more than one mother or father figure. Be sensitive to each child's situation. Some children may have disabilities. Learn about the child's disability. Plan to include the child in all activities and show him the unconditional love of Jesus.

● **Plan to lead children to Jesus.**
Remember that all your plans should lead in only one direction—to Jesus. Plan and pray that all you do will help lay the foundation for a child to have a lifelong relationship with Jesus Christ.

Basic Supplies Needed
Books and equipment
- *NIV* Bibles, white board and dry-erase markers, erasers, bulletin board and pushpins, CD player, stapler, rulers, scissors, hole punch, beanbags

Consumable materials
- markers, crayons, colored pencils, pencils, dry-erase markers, plain paper, card stock, construction paper, roll paper, poster board, index cards, clear tape, glue, reusable adhesive, yarn, staples, craft sticks, paper towels, old magazines, paper fasteners

Bible Skills

As you teach the lessons in this book, you will be helping the kids in your class develop the ability to study God's Word and find for themselves God's answers for the everyday situations they face. Bible skills activities are intentionally integrated into each lesson.

EARLY ELEMENTARY children will . . .

September	Know the Bible has an Old Testament and a New Testament. Understand the difference between the Old Testament and New Testament.
October	Understand what a Scripture reference means.
November	Name Old Testament main characters.
December	Use the table of contents to find a testament.
January	Use the table of contents to find a book.
February	Name New Testament main characters.
March	Review the difference between the Old Testament and New Testament.
April	Review what a Scripture reference means.
May	Name the first four books in the New Testament.
June	Review using a table of contents to find a book.
July	Name the first five books of the Old Testament.
August	Review all Bible skills.
Ongoing Skills	Find verses in the Bible. Begin to read Bible verses. Memorize selected Bible verses.

Leading Kids to Jesus

One of the greatest joys of teaching is the opportunity to participate with kids as they begin thinking about salvation decisions. A "Leading Young Hearts to the Lord" Pocket Guide is included on the *Resources* CD. Print and keep a copy handy so that you will be prepared whenever the opportunity arises to discuss this important matter.

"My Lord, I do not ask to stand, as king or prince of high degree. I only pray that hand-in-hand, a child and I may come to Thee."

—*anonymous*

Jesus Is Special

Special Unit

	Bible Focus	Life Focus
People Praise Jesus	Jesus' triumphal entry. Matthew 21; John 12	❤ Jesus is special; we can praise Him.
Jesus Dies and Lives Again	Jesus' resurrection. John 18–20	❤ Jesus is special; tell everyone He's alive!

Bible Memory
Matthew 28:5, 6

The angel said to the women, "Do not be afraid, for I know that you are looking for Jesus, who was crucified. He is not here; he has risen, just as he said. Come and see the place where he lay."

Print the Additional Bible Memory file from the Resources CD for more Bible Memory verses kids will enjoy learning.

Bible Skill for the Special Unit
Children will
- review the difference between the Old Testament and the New Testament.

Ongoing Bible Skills
Children will
- find verses in the Bible.
- begin to read Bible verses.
- memorize selected Bible verses.

Life Skills for the Special Unit
Children will
- desire to praise Jesus.
- tell others that Jesus is alive.

HeartShaper Materials for the Special Unit
Early Elementary Activities, Triumphal Entry and Jesus' Resurrection
Early Elementary Teaching Pictures, Triumphal Entry and Jesus' Resurrection
Early Elementary Resources
CD
"He Has Risen," Tracks 1, 2
"Jesus Is Special," Track 9
Bible Memory: Additional Bible Memory for Special Unit (*NIV* and *KJV*), Bible Memory for Special Unit (*NIV* and *KJV*)
Bible Skills Worksheets, Special Unit
Buzzy Bee Letters, TE and JR Lessons
Worship Time Ideas, Special Unit
Review Questions, Special Unit
Letter to Families, Special Unit
Posters and Activities: "Jesus Is Special" rhythm activity (words), books of the Old Testament and New Testament posters
Teacher Helps: Attendance Chart, Celebrate the Resurrection of Jesus, Early Elementary Children, Leading Young Hearts Pocket Guide, Make the Most of Your Room, Some Things Should Never Change!, A Teacher's To-Do List, Lesson Plan Outline, Transition Tips, Easels and Supports
Visuals
Sheet 1 Bible Memory poster, story figures TEa–TEe and palm leaves; Sheet 2 story figures JRa–JRi and easels
Weekly Bible Reader® Issue TE (Triumphal Entry), Issue JR (Jesus' Resurrection), and the Special Issue
Faith & Family online resource
A weekly devotional guide for parents and kids to use together. Go to www.heartshaper.com.

Teaching Tips
❤ Introduce guests and tell them how glad you are they came. Make sure new children know your name and what will happen in class. You may want to ask a few children to serve as special friends to new children.

❤ When children need to work in pairs or small groups, you can vary how this is done, but never make a child feel left out or uncomfortable. Every child who comes into your class should feel the love and acceptance of Christ.

Additional Activities for this Unit

Use these activities for early arrivers, for children who finish activities quickly, and when you are waiting for parents to arrive.

"Jesus Is Special" Bulletin Board

Title a bulletin board "Jesus is special because . . ." Have children draw shapes (triangles, circles, rectangles, squares) and cut them out. They should use each shape to trace and cut out a matching shape. Guide the children to print on one of their shapes a way Jesus is special. On the matching shape, the kids should draw a picture of what they wrote. Put the two shapes together with the picture on top and mount the shapes on the bulletin board. Leave the shapes on top free at the bottoms, so that kids can lift the pictures and read the messages underneath.

Fun Snack Idea

Let children ice and decorate cookies in the shapes of hearts and crosses. Be sure that each child gets one heart-shaped and one cross-shaped cookie. As kids work, talk about the love Jesus had for us (heart-shaped cookies) that led Him to die for us on the cross (cross-shaped cookies).

Make Maracas

Give each child a bag to decorate with markers. Have each child scoop about a cup of dried beans or uncooked popcorn into a plastic container or empty aluminum can. Tape on the lid or tape the opening closed on the can. Kids can place the container in the bottom of their bags. Use yarn to tie a handle on the bag to form a maraca. Kids can use the maracas while they sing songs about Jesus and His resurrection.

Sweet Messages

Let kids make these sweet messages to give to friends and family members. Write or type the following and copy onto colorful paper: "You are 'egg-stra' special to Jesus!" Provide candy in the shape of an egg. Let kids put the candy in resealable bags and attach the papers to the bags. You could also have the kids make extra bags to give to other classes or to guests you have in your class.

Bible Skills

Make copies of the Bible Skills Worksheets for the Special Unit from the *Resources* CD. For the Special Unit, children will review the difference between the Old Testament and the New Testament.

Teaching Tip
For more snack, song, game, and project ideas, see the article, "Celebrate the Resurrection of Jesus," found in the Teacher Helps folder on the *Resources* CD.

People Praise Jesus

Bible Focus: Matthew 21:1-11; John 12:12-19

Bible Memory: The angel said to the women, "Do not be afraid, for I know that you are looking for Jesus, who was crucified. He is not here; he has risen, just as he said. Come and see the place where he lay" (Matthew 28:5, 6).

Life Focus: ♥ Jesus is special; we can praise Him.

Heart to Heart

The praises the people said to Jesus in Matthew 21:9 were true—"Hosanna to the Son of David!" Jesus was a descendant of David. "Blessed is he who comes in the name of the Lord!" God had blessed Jesus, and Jesus certainly was doing everything in the name of the Lord. "Hosanna in the highest heaven!" Nothing but praise would do for this king. Remember to do some praising yourself this week. Give Jesus the praises He is worthy of.

Lesson at a Glance

		HeartShaper Materials	Other Materials
Step 1 **Focus In** Use one of these activities to help children *explore what* special means.	*Quick Step* Which Is Special?	• none	• none
	Option Special Drawings	• none	• paper, markers
	Bible Memory *Use this activity to introduce the Bible Memory verses.*	• *Resources* Sheet 1 Bible Memory poster	• Bible, reusable adhesive
Step 2 **Explore His Word** Use all of these activities to help children *tell how the people praised Jesus for being special* and develop Bible skills.	People Praise Jesus **Bible Review Activity** **Bible Skill Builder and Bible Memory Activity**	• reproducible p. 89; *Resources* Sheet 1 story figures TEa–TEe and palm leaves, CD including the Review Questions printable file; *Teaching Picture* Triumphal Entry; *Activities* p. 3	• white board, dry-erase marker, Bibles, green card stock or construction paper, marker, scissors, reusable adhesive, jumbo craft sticks, clear tape or glue, CD player
Step 3 **Make It Real** Use one of these activities to help children *discover reasons to praise Jesus for being special.*	*Quick Step* Palm Leaves Praise	• none	• palm leaves used in the Bible story
	Option Change Places!	• none	• white board, dry-erase marker, paper, pencils
	Option Story from *Weekly Bible Reader®*	• *Weekly Bible Reader®* Issue TE	• none
Step 4 **Live It Out** Use one of these activities to help children *praise Jesus for being special.*	*Quick Step* "Jesus Is Special"	• *Resources* CD	• CD player
	Option Praying Praise	• none	• none
	Saying Good-bye	• *Weekly Bible Reader®* Issue TE, *Activities* p. 2 Special Unit Bible Memory poster and stickers	• none

Life Focus

♥ Jesus is special; we can praise Him.

Step 1 • Use one of these activities to help children **explore what** *special* **means.**
Use the Bible Memory activity to introduce the memory verses.

Welcome

- Welcome each child by name.
- Do check-in procedures you follow (name and security tags, offering, attendance chart, etc.).
- Early arrivers will enjoy doing one or more of the activities described on page 6.

Quick Step   Which Is Special?

Let's think about what the word *special* means. Tell the children that you will name two things that are similar and they will decide which is special.
1. **A huge, three-layer birthday cake with ice cream or a plain cupcake. If you think the birthday cake is special, stand.** (pause so kids can stand) **If you think the cupcake is special, stand.** 2. **One hour playing in your yard or a weeklong vacation to a theme park. If you think playing in your yard is special, stand. If you think the vacation is special, stand.**
3. **One balloon or 100 balloons. If you think 1 balloon is special, stand. If you think 100 balloons are special, stand.** 4. **Going to a major league baseball game or going to a little league game. If you think the major league game is special, stand. If you think the little league game is special, stand.**
- **What makes something special?** (it's unusual; it's great; it's better than ordinary)
There are lots of special things. We're going to discover that because ♥ **Jesus is special, we can praise Him.**

Materials
none

Action

Added Fun!
Let kids name pairs of special and ordinary things for the rest of the class to decide which is special.

Option   Special Drawings

What do you think the word *special* means? (Accept the children's responses.) Distribute the paper and markers. **I want you to draw three things. Draw a picture of a food you think is special, an activity you think is special, and a person you think is special.** When everyone is done, have kids show their pictures and tell about what they drew. Ask kids these questions:
- **Why is that food special?**
- **Why is that activity special?**
- **Why is that person special?**
- **What makes something special?** (it's unusual; it's great; it's better than ordinary)
There are lots of special things. We're going to discover that because ♥ **Jesus is special, we can praise Him.**

Materials
paper, markers

Art

Bible Memory   Matthew 28:5, 6

As I read Matthew 28:5 and 6, listen for who is special. Read Matthew 28:5, 6 aloud from the Bible. **Who is special?** (Jesus) **Why is Jesus special?** (He died but came back to life.) Display the Bible Memory poster. Read the words while pointing to the words and pictures. Read again and invite kids to say the Bible Memory verses with you. **Jesus dying for us and then coming back to life makes Him very special!** ♥ **Jesus is special; we can praise Him!**

Materials
Bible, *Resources* Sheet 1 Bible Memory poster, reusable adhesive

Memorize

Transition to Explore His Word
See the *Resources* CD Transition Tips printable file. As children gather, make sure you have all the materials you need.

Life Focus

❤ Jesus is special; we can praise Him.

Explore His Word (20 minutes)

Step 2 • Use all of these activities to help children **tell how the people praised Jesus for being special** and develop Bible skills.

Bible Background for the Teacher

This event is often referred to as the triumphal entry. It was a festive welcoming of Jesus to the city, much like a parade for a hero coming to town. The city was packed at this time because Jewish people from many nations had traveled to Jerusalem to celebrate the Passover Feast, the holiday memorializing God's rescue of His people from Egypt.

Jesus chose to ride into town on a donkey, just as King David and his sons did. This fulfilled a prophecy about how the Messiah would enter Jerusalem (Zechariah 9:9). A king who entered a town on a donkey was saying "I come in peace."

Palm branches were waved as a sign of rejoicing. Palm branches had also been associated with Israel's victories in battle. This is important because the Jewish people were under the rule of Rome. They saw Jesus as the promised Messiah or Savior. The crowd called Him "Son of David" which was a title for the coming Messiah. They shouted "Hosanna!" which means "save now." The problem was that they saw Jesus as one who would save them from the harsh Roman government. They didn't realize that Jesus' mission was to save all people from an even harsher ruler—sin, and its punishment, eternal separation from God.

Worship Time

If you want to offer a time of worship, see the *Resources* CD Worship Time Ideas printable file for suggestions.

Materials

white board, dry-erase marker, Bibles, palm leaves (reproducible p. 89, green card stock or construction paper, jumbo craft sticks, marker, scissors, clear tape or glue), *Resources* Sheet 1 story figures TEa–TEe, reusable adhesive, *Teaching Picture* Triumphal Entry

Before Class

You may want to make a palm leaf for each child. Decide how you want to display the story figures during the story. You could attach easels, craft sticks, or paper tubes to the backs of figures.

People Praise Jesus   (Matthew 21:1-11; John 12:12-19)

The Bible is divided into two main sections. What are they? (Old and New Testaments) **The Bible story comes from the New Testament books of Matthew and John.** Write "John 12:12" on the board. **Let's find the book of John in the New Testament.** Tell kids to find the table of contents in the front of their Bibles and find the book of John. Help the children turn to John 12:12 in their Bibles and ask for a volunteer to read the verse.

Distribute the palm leaves or have kids make the palm leaves now. **I need you to help tell today's Bible story. You're going to be part of the crowd in the city of Jerusalem. When I ask you to, stand and wave your palm leaves. And you're going to repeat some of the things the crowd says. Get ready because something exciting is about to happen! Listen for how the people praised Jesus.**

(Have your Bible open to Matthew 21. Display the story figures as indicated.) Jesus *(TEa)* and His followers were coming near the city of Jerusalem. Jesus sent two of His followers *(TEb)* into a village. He told them they would find a donkey tied there with its young donkey, called a colt. They were to untie them and bring them to Jesus. The followers did what Jesus told them to do. They found the donkey and its colt and took them to Jesus. His followers laid their coats on the donkey and its colt, and Jesus sat on the colt *(put TEd on TEc)*.

People in Jerusalem heard that Jesus was coming. A great crowd of people gathered to see Jesus *(TEe)*. The people had heard and may have seen some of the wonderful things that Jesus had done—making people who were blind see and people who were deaf hear. Many people knew Jesus had made a man named Lazarus come back to life. Maybe Jesus had helped some of the people in the crowd too. They were very excited to see Jesus.

Jesus rode on the colt into Jerusalem. Many people took branches from palm trees and went out to meet Jesus. The people spread their coats and palm branches on the road before Him *(lay down the palm leaves)*. Some walked ahead of Jesus. Some walked behind Him.

(Have kids stand, wave their palm leaves, and repeat what the people

said.) They shouted, "Hosanna to the Son of David! Blessed is he who comes in the name of the Lord! Hosanna in the highest heaven!" (Matthew 21:9).

The crowd of people continued praising Jesus as He went into Jerusalem. The city was filled with excitement. Some of the people asked, "Who is this man?" *(Have the kids repeat.)*

Some of the other people answered, "This is Jesus. He is from Nazareth, and He is a prophet." *(Have the kids repeat; show* Teaching Picture *Triumphal Entry.)*

Bible Review Activity

How did the people praise Jesus? (They spread their coats and palm branches on the road in front of Him. They shouted "Hosanna!" They called Jesus the Son of David and praised Him.) **Let's make some puppets that will help us remember the story.** Distribute the activity pages, scissors, tape or glue, and craft sticks. Read the directions aloud and help children as needed to make the puppets, attaching craft sticks to the backs of the figures. Encourage the children to use their figures to act out the story as you retell it. Invite them to also say the words the crowd said.

After the story, ask the following questions. Kids should respond by holding up the correct figures. Use the Review Questions from the CD for more questions about the story.

• **Whom did Jesus tell to go into Jerusalem to find a donkey?** (two followers)

• **On what did Jesus ride into Jerusalem?** (colt)

• **Who shouted "Hosanna to the Son of David"?** (the people)

• **What did the people wave to praise Jesus?** (palm leaves)

• **Whom did the people praise?** (Jesus)

The people praised Jesus. Since ♥ Jesus is special, we can praise Him too!

Materials
Activities p. 3, scissors, craft sticks, clear tape or glue, *Resources* CD Review Questions printable file

Bible Skill Builder and Bible Memory Activity

Ask the children to turn to the table of contents in the front of their Bibles. **Look at the table of contents. Into what two main sections is the Bible divided?** (Old and New Testaments) **In which section do we read about God making the world?** (Old) **In which section do we read about Jesus coming to earth to be our Savior?** (New) Write "Matthew 28:5, 6" on the board. **Look in the table of contents to find the book of Matthew.** Give kids time to find it. **Is Matthew in the Old or New Testament?** (New) Guide children to turn to Matthew 28:5, 6 in their Bibles and ask for volunteers to read the verses.

Play "He Has Risen." Play the song again and invite kids to join in. Kids will enjoy doing these motions while singing the song: *afraid*—cross the arms with hands open; *Jesus*—touch the middle finger of one hand to the middle of the palm of the other hand and then repeat with the other hand; *risen*—raise both arms; *alive*—move both hands up from the waist to the neck; *lay*—spread both arms with palms open.

One of the main things that makes Jesus special is that He rose from the dead. Since ♥ Jesus is special, we can praise Him!

Materials
Bibles, white board, dry-erase marker, *Resources* CD Tracks 1 and 2, CD player

Teaching Tip
Print and use the Special Unit Bible Skills Worksheets found on the *Resources* CD to help children review the difference between the Old Testament and the New Testament.

Life Focus

❤ Jesus is special; we can praise Him.

Make It Real (15 minutes)

Step 3 • Use one of these activities to help children **discover reasons to praise Jesus for being special.**

Materials

palm leaves used in the Bible story

Expert Tip

"When you state your behavior guidelines in a positive way, your students are less likely to tune you out."

—*Jody Capehart*

Materials

white board, dry-erase marker, paper, pencils

Added Fun!

After a couple of rounds, have kids exchange papers and continue playing.

Materials

Weekly Bible Reader® Issue TE

═══ *Quick Step* Palm Leaves Praise

We've learned that the people praised Jesus and that since ❤ **Jesus is special, we can praise Him too! Let's discover reasons to praise Jesus for being special.** Tell the kids that as you read each sentence about Jesus, they are to decide if it is a reason to praise Jesus. Kids should wave their palm leaves if the sentence tells a reason to praise Jesus. (Hint: All the sentences are reasons to praise Jesus.)

We can praise Jesus for being special because He died on the cross.
We can praise Jesus for being special because He rose from the dead.
We can praise Jesus for being special because He did miracles.
We can praise Jesus for being special because He is the Son of God.
We can praise Jesus for being special because He loves us.
We can praise Jesus for being special because He is powerful.
• Can you think of some other reasons to praise Jesus for being special?

There are lots of reasons to praise Jesus for being special. Since ❤ **Jesus is special, we can praise Him!**

Option   Change Places!

We've learned that the people praised Jesus and that since ❤ **Jesus is special, we can praise Him too! What are some reasons to praise Jesus for being special?** As children give reasons, list them on the board. (He died on the cross. He rose from the dead. He did miracles. He is the Son of God. He loves us. He is powerful.) Distribute the paper and pencils. Ask kids to write on their papers one of the reasons to praise Jesus.

Ask the kids to hold their papers and sit in a circle. You can stand in the middle of the circle. Call out two or three of the reasons to praise Jesus and then say "Change places!" The children who have those reasons written on their papers are to change places with each other before you (or the person in the middle) can sit in one of their places. Whoever is left without a place to sit can be in the middle and call out a few reasons to praise Jesus. Play as time permits.

There are lots of reasons to praise Jesus for being special. Since ❤ **Jesus is special, we can praise Him!**

Option   Story from *Weekly Bible Reader®*

We've learned that the people praised Jesus and that since ❤ **Jesus is special, we can praise Him too! Let's discover reasons to praise Jesus for being special.** Read "The Crowd Went Wild."
• What are some reasons to praise Jesus for being special? (See the activities above for possible responses.)

There are lots of reasons to praise Jesus for being special. Since ❤ **Jesus is special, we can praise Him!**

Live It Out (10 minutes)

Step 4 • Use one of these activities to help children **praise Jesus for being special.**

≡ *Quick Step* "Jesus Is Special"

Since we know that ❤ Jesus is special, we can praise Him! So let's praise Him now! Play "Jesus Is Special." Play again and invite kids to join you. The children will enjoy doing the following motions while doing this rhythm activity: *Jesus*—touch the middle finger of one hand to the middle of the palm of the other hand and then repeat with the other hand; *yes*—shake a closed fist up and down; *come*—the index fingers on both hands move toward the body; *praise Him*—clap hands on each word; *tell*—the index finger starts under the chin and is thrust outward; *alive*—move both hands up from the waist to the neck.

Close with a time of prayer. Encourage all children to pray aloud and praise Jesus for being special.

Materials
Resources CD Track 9, CD player

Added Fun!
Let kids play rhythm instruments while doing the rhythm activity.

Option Praying Praise

Since we know that ❤ Jesus is special, we can praise Him! So let's praise Him now with our prayers. Have the children gather for a time of prayer. Tell kids that you will pray, thanking Jesus for being special. After each sentence prayer, they are to respond by praying "You are special."

We praise You, Jesus, for dying on the cross. Pause while kids respond: You are special. **We praise You, Jesus, for rising from the dead.** Kids respond: You are special. **We praise You, Jesus, for loving us.** Kids respond: You are special. **We praise You, Jesus, because You did miracles.** Kids respond: You are special. **We praise You, Jesus, because You are powerful.** Kids respond: You are special. **We praise You, Jesus, because You are the Son of God.** Kids respond: You are special. **We praise You, Jesus. You are special.** Kids respond: You are special. **In Jesus' name, amen.**

Materials
none

Saying Good-bye

• Distribute the Triumphal Entry Issue of *Weekly Bible Reader*® and the *Activities* page 2 Special Unit Bible Memory poster and stickers. Stickers are in the middle of *Early Elementary Activities*. Encourage kids to complete their posters at home.

• Make sure children have projects and activity sheets they have done.

• If you have time before parents arrive, use some of the activities on page 6.

• Be sure parents know about the *Faith & Family* page available online to download and use at home. You may want to print and have a copy on display for parents to see. Go to www.heartshaper.com.

Evaluate
• How eager were the children to praise Jesus?
• Did you allow enough time for children to complete an activity before switching to another activity?

Jesus Dies and Lives Again

Special Unit
See the table of contents

Bible Focus: John 18:1-4, 24, 28–20:18

Bible Memory: The angel said to the women, "Do not be afraid, for I know that you are looking for Jesus, who was crucified. He is not here; he has risen, just as he said. Come and see the place where he lay" (Matthew 28:5, 6).

Life Focus: ❤ Jesus is special; tell everyone He's alive!

Heart to Heart

This week you have the privilege of sharing with the children in your class the excitement of the resurrection! That means that you must first become excited about the news of the resurrection. Catch the wonder of that morning by imagining yourself as Mary visiting the empty tomb. Reflect this week on the overwhelming joys of forgiven sin and new life. Then, like Mary, go and tell the children in your class the real reason for the celebration: Jesus is alive!

Lesson at a Glance

		HeartShaper Materials	Other Materials
Step 1 **Focus In** Use one of these activities to help children *explore alive and dead.*	*Quick Step* Alive and Dead *Activity Page*	• *Activities* p. 5	• colored pencils or crayons
	Option Is He Alive? *Object Lesson*	• none	• stethoscope, mirror, snack
	Bible Memory *Use this activity to introduce the Bible Memory verses.* *Memorize*	• *Resources* Sheet 1 Bible Memory poster	• Bible, reusable adhesive
Step 2 **Explore His Word** Use all of these activities to help children *tell how Jesus showed He is special* and develop Bible skills.	Jesus Dies and Lives Again *Bible Story*	• *Resources* Sheet 2 story figures JRa–JRi and easels, CD; *Teaching Picture* Jesus' Resurrection	• white board, dry-erase marker, Bibles, clear tape, reusable adhesive, plastic eggs, small crosses or pieces of wood, small stones, paper, markers, CD player
	Bible Review Activity *Craft*		
	Bible Skill Builder and Bible Memory Activity *Music*		
Step 3 **Make It Real** Use one of these activities to help children *discover ways to tell that Jesus is alive.*	*Quick Step* How Can You Tell? *Activity Page*	• *Activities* p. 6	• pencils
	Option That's a Way *Game*	• none	• none
	Option Story from *Weekly Bible Reader* *Listen*	• *Weekly Bible Reader®* Issue JR	• none
Step 4 **Live It Out** Use one of these activities to help children *plan a way to tell someone that Jesus is alive.*	*Quick Step* Resurrection Card *Art*	• reproducible p. 90	• scissors, markers or colored pencils
	Option Story Eggs *Action*	• *Resources* CD	• story eggs made in Step 2, CD player
	Saying Good-bye	• *Weekly Bible Reader®* Issue JR and the Special Issue	• none

Focus In (15 minutes)

Step 1 • Use one of these activities to help children **explore alive and dead.** Use the Bible Memory activity to introduce the memory verses.

Welcome
- Welcome each child by name.
- Do check-in procedures you follow (name and security tags, offering, attendance chart, etc.).
- Early arrivers will enjoy doing one or more of the activities described on page 6.

☰ *Quick Step* Alive and Dead

Today we're going to explore things that are alive and things that are dead. What are some things that are alive? (Accept children's responses.) **What are some things that are dead?** Distribute the activity pages and colored pencils or crayons. Read the directions aloud and let children complete their pages. When finished, let the children share what they drew.
- **How do you know when a flower is alive?** (pretty color, leaves are green, smells good)
- **How do you know when an animal is alive?** (walks or runs, eats, breathes)
- **How do you know when a person is alive?** (has a heartbeat and pulse, breathes, talks, eats)

Today we're going to learn about someone who was dead but then came alive!

Materials

Activities p. 5, colored pencils or crayons

Activity Page

Added Fun!

Let kids draw other things that are alive and things that are dead.

Option   Is He Alive?

Today we're going to explore things that are alive and things that are dead. Let's explore how we can know that a person is alive. Ask for a volunteer. **Let's see if this person is alive.** Listen to her heartbeat with the stethoscope. Check her pulse. Put the mirror under her nose and see if there's breath coming from her nose. Then offer her a snack to eat.
- **Is this person alive? How do you know?** (She has a heartbeat, a pulse, is breathing, and ate food.)

Let children have fun listening to heartbeats, feeling pulses, putting the mirror under their noses, and eating a snack.
- **How do you know when someone is dead?** (no heartbeat, no pulse, no breathing, can't eat)

Today we're going to learn about someone who was dead but then came alive!

Materials

stethoscope, mirror, snack

Object Lesson

Bible Memory   Matthew 28:5, 6

Our Bible Memory verses tell us something very special about Jesus. Listen for what's so special about Jesus. Read Matthew 28:5, 6 from the Bible. **What's special about Jesus?** (He rose from the dead.) Display the Bible Memory poster. Encourage the children to join you in reading the words while you point to the words and pictures. Divide the class into three groups. Have one group say the first sentence, another group say the second sentence, and the remaining group say the third sentence. Lead the groups in saying their verses in order three times, a little louder each time. **Jesus dying for us and then coming back to life makes Him very special! We want to tell everyone what Jesus has done. Since ♥ Jesus is special, tell everyone He's alive!**

Materials

Bible, *Resources* Sheet 1 Bible Memory poster, reusable adhesive

Memorize

Transition to Explore His Word

See the *Resources* CD Transition Tips printable file. As children gather, make sure you have all the materials you need.

Life Focus

♥ Jesus is special; tell everyone He's alive.

Explore His Word (20 minutes)

Step 2 • Use all of these activities to help children **tell how Jesus showed He is special** and develop Bible skills.

Bible Background for the Teacher

Since the Jews were living under the rule of the Roman government, they could not legally execute someone without Rome's permission. That's why they had to pressure the Roman ruler, Pilate, to sentence Jesus to death.

A tomb was a cave-like opening carved in a rock. It was Jewish tradition at that time to wrap a body in linen strips, treat it with spices and ointments, and then place the body in a tomb so that it would not be disturbed.

John records only Mary Magdalene at the tomb while the other three Gospels record other women also present. Perhaps Mary came first and the other women came later. We do not know why Mary did not at first recognize Jesus. Mary may not have recognized Jesus at first because she was crying and filled with grief. Or Jesus may have intentionally prevented recognition. Or Jesus may have looked different.

Why did Jesus have to die? Why didn't He use His God-powers to fight back? John 10:17, 18 tells us that Jesus died willingly. He knew He was coming to earth to die, to pay the penalty for our sins so that anyone who believes in Him can be at peace with God and live with Him forever (John 3:16).

Worship Time

If you want to offer a time of worship, see the *Resources* CD Worship Time Ideas printable file for suggestions.

Materials

white board, dry-erase marker, Bibles, *Resources* Sheet 2 story figures JRa–JRi and easels, clear tape, reusable adhesive, *Teaching Picture* Jesus' Resurrection

Before Class

Attach the easels to the backs of the figures. Or you could attach craft sticks or paper tubes to the backs of figures. Or you may want to display the figures on a wall, a piece of poster board, or a bulletin board.

Jesus Dies and Lives Again (John 18:1-4, 24, 28–20:18)

The Bible story comes from the book of John. Write "John 18:1" on the board. **The book of John tells about Jesus and His life. Do you think the book of John is in the Old Testament or New Testament?** (New) **Why do you think it's in the New Testament?** (The New Testament tells about Jesus and His life.) Tell kids to find the table of contents in the front of their Bibles and find the book of John. Help kids turn to John 18:1 in their Bibles and ask for a volunteer to read the verse.

You can help tell today's Bible story. When you hear me say a sentence that begins with "something had happened," you need to repeat that sentence after me. And you need to listen for how Jesus showed He is special.

(Have your Bible open to John 18. Display the story figures as indicated.) Jesus *(JRa)* had been teaching the people for three years. He had done miracles and had taught His followers many things about God and how they should live. Although many people loved Jesus, there were also people who hated Him, who didn't believe in Him, and who wanted Him dead.

One evening when Jesus was with His followers in a garden, soldiers and guards came to arrest Him. Jesus was put on trial before the Roman governor named Pilate. Pilate said that Jesus had done nothing wrong. But the Jewish leaders insisted that Jesus must be killed. And so Pilate passed the death sentence on Jesus and turned Him over to Roman soldiers *(JRb)*. They nailed Jesus to a cross and He died *(JRc)*. Something had happened, something very bad. *(Kids repeat: Something had happened, something very bad.)*

Nicodemus and Joseph of Arimathea took Jesus' body. The men wrapped Jesus' body in strips of cloth and put His body in a tomb *(JRd)*. A large stone was rolled over the entrance to the tomb *(JRe)*. Something had happened, something very sad. *(Kids repeat: Something had happened, something very sad.)*

Very early Sunday morning, three days after Jesus had died, Mary Magdalene *(JRf)* went to the tomb. It was still dark, but Mary could see that the huge stone had been moved away from the entrance to the tomb. Mary ran to tell Peter *(JRg)*

and John *(JRh)*. Mary told them, "They have taken the body of Jesus from the tomb, and we don't know where they have put Him." Something had happened, but what was it? *(Kids repeat: Something had happened, but what was it?)*

Peter and John ran to the tomb and looked inside. Jesus was gone!

Later Mary cried as she stood outside the tomb. Mary looked inside the tomb. There were two angels dressed in white!

The angels asked, "Why are you crying?"

Mary answered, "They have taken away my Lord. I don't know where He is." Something had happened, but what was it? *(Kids repeat: Something had happened, but what was it?)*

Mary turned around and saw Jesus standing close by but she didn't recognize Him *(JRi)*. She thought He was the gardener.

Jesus asked, "Why are you crying?"

Mary asked, "Did you take the body of Jesus? Tell me where you have taken Him, and I will get Him" *(show* Teaching Picture *Jesus' Resurrection)*.

Jesus said to her, "Mary."

Mary then knew the man was Jesus! Jesus told Mary to go back to His followers and tell them what she had seen. Mary did tell Jesus' followers that she had seen the Lord. Jesus is alive! Something had happened; Jesus is alive! *(Kids repeat: Something had happened; Jesus is alive!)*

Bible Review Activity

How did Jesus show He is special? (He did miracles. He died on the cross but rose from the dead.) **We're going to make story eggs that will remind us that Jesus rose from the dead.** Give each child four plastic eggs.

• **What happened first in the story?** (Jesus died on a cross.) Have kids put the crosses or pieces of wood into one of their eggs.

• **What happened next?** (His body was put in a tomb and a stone rolled over the entrance.) Have kids put the stones in another egg.

• **What happened on the third day after Jesus was put in the tomb?** (Mary went to the tomb and found Jesus' body was gone. Mary saw Jesus alive.) Tell kids not to put anything in the third egg, since Jesus' tomb was empty.

• **What happened after Mary saw Jesus alive?** (She went to tell Jesus' followers. She said, "I have seen the Lord!")

Explain that what Mary said is like saying "Jesus is alive!" Have children write "Jesus is alive!" on the strips of paper and put them in their fourth egg. **Your story eggs will remind you that since ♥ Jesus is special, tell everyone He's alive!**

Materials
4 refillable, plastic eggs for each child; small crosses or smooth pieces of wood; small stones; small strips of paper; markers

Craft

Added Fun!
Let kids decorate the eggs with stickers of Jesus, the cross, and the empty tomb.

Bible Skill Builder and Bible Memory Activity

Write "Old Testament" on one side of the board, "New Testament" on the other side of the board, and "Matthew 28:5, 6" between them. **Turn to the table of contents in the front of your Bibles and find the book of Matthew. Raise your hand when you know whether Matthew is in the Old Testament or New Testament.** Give all children time to find it. Choose a child to come to the board and draw a line from Matthew 28:5, 6 to either the Old Testament or New Testament. (New) **Who does the New Testament tell about?** (Jesus) Guide children to turn to Matthew 28:5, 6 in their Bibles and ask for volunteers to read the verses.

Play "He Has Risen" and encourage kids to join in singing. Kids will enjoy doing the motions described in the Step 2 Bible Skill Builder and Bible Memory Activity on page 10. **Since ♥ Jesus is special, tell everyone He's alive!**

Materials
Bibles, white board, dry-erase marker, *Resources* CD Tracks 1 and 2, CD player

Music

Teaching Tip
Print and use the Special Unit Bible Skills Worksheets found on the *Resources* CD to help children review the difference between the Old Testament and the New Testament.

Life Focus
❤ Jesus is special; tell everyone He's alive.

Make It Real (15 minutes)

Step 3 • Use one of these activities to help children **discover ways to tell that Jesus is alive.**

Materials
Activities p. 6, pencils

Added Fun!
Have each kid name something and the rest of the class can tell whether it is a way to tell about Jesus or not.

Activity Page

Materials
none

Game

Teaching Tip
If children respond "yes" on some of the *no* statements, ask them to explain their responses. They may be able to validate their answers.

Materials
Weekly Bible Reader®
Issue JR

LISTEN

☰ *Quick Step* How Can You Tell?
We've learned that Jesus showed He was special by coming back to life after He had been crucified. Let's discover some ways to tell others that Jesus is alive. Distribute the activity pages and pencils. Read the directions aloud. Ask for volunteers to read the words on each tomb opening and decide if it's a way to tell others about Jesus.
- **To whom could you tell the Bible Memory verses?**
- **To whom could you sing a song about Jesus?**
- **What friend could you tell that Jesus is alive?**
- **To whom could you give a card about Jesus coming back to life?**
- **What are some other ways you could tell that Jesus is alive?**

There are lots of ways to tell others that Jesus is alive. Since ❤ Jesus is special, tell everyone He's alive!

Option   That's a Way
We've learned that Jesus showed He was special by coming back to life after He had been crucified. Let's discover some ways to tell others that Jesus is alive. Tell the children that you will read some sentences. If a sentence is a way they can tell others that Jesus is alive, they should jump up and shout "Yes, that's a way." If a sentence is not a way to tell others that Jesus is alive, they should stay seated and whisper "No, that's not a way."

You can tell that Jesus is alive by singing a song about Jesus. (yes)
You can tell that Jesus is alive by telling a friend the Bible Memory verses. (yes)
You can tell that Jesus is alive by playing soccer. (no)
You can tell that Jesus is alive by drawing a picture of Jesus in front of an empty tomb. (yes)
You can tell that Jesus is alive by going shopping. (no)
You can tell that Jesus is alive by making a card about Jesus' life and giving it to someone. (yes)
You can tell that Jesus is alive by telling the Bible story about Jesus dying on the cross and rising from the dead. (yes)

There are lots of ways to tell others that Jesus is alive. Since ❤ Jesus is special, tell everyone He's alive!

Option   Story from *Weekly Bible Reader®*
We've learned that Jesus showed He was special by coming back to life after He had been crucified. Let's discover some ways to tell others that Jesus is alive. Read "Tell Me More."
- **What are some ways to tell others that Jesus is alive?** (See the activities above for possible responses.)

There are lots of ways to tell others that Jesus is alive. Since ❤ Jesus is special, tell everyone He's alive!

Life Focus
♥ Jesus is special; tell everyone He's alive.

Step 4 • Use one of these activities to help children **plan a way to tell someone that Jesus is alive.**

≡ *Quick Step* Resurrection Card

Since we know that ♥ Jesus is special, we need to tell everyone He's alive! One way to tell others that Jesus is alive is to make a card about Him to give to someone. Before class, make copies of the reproducible page. Distribute the reproducible pages, scissors, and markers. Tell kids to be thinking about who they want to give their cards to as they work on them. Read aloud the words on the card. Kids can color the cards and write any other messages they would like to, such as "Jesus loves you." Then the children can color the cards and cut them out. Help kids as necessary to fold their cards.

Have the children bring their completed cards to a closing prayer time. Ask kids to share whom they plan on giving their cards to. Encourage all children to pray and thank God that Jesus is alive.

Materials
reproducible p. 90, scissors, markers or colored pencils

Art

Option Story Eggs

Since we know that ♥ Jesus is special, we need to tell everyone He's alive! One way to tell others that Jesus is alive is to share with them the story eggs you made. If children did not make the story eggs in the Step 2 Bible Review Activity, let them do so now.

Tell or review with children what the objects in their eggs mean. Then divide children into pairs or small groups. Ask children to use their eggs to tell each other about the resurrection of Jesus. Tell kids that they can use their story eggs to tell others that Jesus is alive.

Play "Jesus Is Special" and invite kids to join in. Kids will enjoy doing the motions found in the Step 4 *Quick Step* activity on page 12.

Close with a time of prayer. Tell the children that you will pray, praising and thanking God that Jesus is alive. After each sentence prayer, they are to respond by praying "I will tell others."

Thank You, God, that Jesus came to earth. Kids respond: I will tell others. **We praise You, God, that Jesus died on the cross because He loves us.** Kids respond: I will tell others. **We praise You, God, that Jesus rose from the dead.** Kids respond: I will tell others. **Since Jesus is special, we want to tell everyone.** Kids respond: I will tell others. **In Jesus' name, amen.**

Materials
story eggs made in Step 2, *Resources* CD Track 9, CD player

Action

Saying Good-bye

• Distribute both the Jesus' Resurrection Issue and the Special Issue of *Weekly Bible Reader*®.
• Make sure children have projects and activity sheets they have done.
• If you have time before parents arrive, use some of the activities on page 6.
• Remind parents that a weekly *Faith & Family* page is available online to print and use with their child at home. See www.heartshaper.com.

Evaluate
• How willing are the children to tell others about Jesus?
• How did you help guests feel welcome?

Jesus Does Great Things

	Bible Focus	**Life Focus**
Lesson 1 Jesus Heals an Official's Son	Jesus heals a sick boy. John 4	❤ Jesus can do great things.
Lesson 2 Jesus Heals a Man at a Pool	Jesus heals a man at a pool. John 5	❤ Jesus can do miracles.
Lesson 3 Jesus Feeds 5,000	Jesus feeds a crowd. John 6	❤ Jesus can give you what you need.
Lesson 4 Jesus Walks on Water	Jesus walks on water. Matthew 14	❤ Jesus can do anything.
Lesson 5 Jesus Brings a Young Man Back to Life	Jesus raises a widow's son. Luke 7	❤ Jesus can make people live again.
Lesson 6 Jesus Heals Jairus's Daughter	Jesus heals Jairus's daughter. Mark 5	❤ Jesus can do great things.

Bible Memory

John 20:30, 31

Jesus performed many other signs in the presence of his disciples, which are not recorded in this book. But these are written that you may believe that Jesus is the Messiah, the Son of God.

Print the Additional Bible Memory file from the Resources CD for more Bible Memory verses kids will enjoy learning.

Bible Skill for Unit 1

Children will

- review what a Scripture reference means.

Ongoing Bible Skills

Children will

- find verses in the Bible.
- begin to read Bible verses.
- memorize selected Bible verses.

Life Skills for Unit 1

Children will

- tell others about Jesus.
- thank Jesus.
- worship and praise Jesus.

HeartShaper Materials for Unit 1

Early Elementary Activities, **Lessons 1–6 and the Unit 1 Bible Memory Poster and Stickers**

Early Elementary Teaching Pictures, **Lessons 1–6**

Early Elementary Resources

CD

"Jesus Can Do Great Things," Tracks 3, 4

"John 20:30, 31," Tracks 5, 6

Bible Story for Lesson 5, Track 12

Bible Story for Lesson 6, Track 13

Bible Memory: Additional Bible Memory for Unit 1 (*NIV* and *KJV*), Bible Memory for Unit 1 (*NIV* and *KJV*)

Bible Skills Worksheets, Unit 1

Buzzy Bee Letters, Lessons 1–6

Worship Time Ideas, Unit 1

Review Questions, Unit 1

Letter to Families, Unit 1

Posters and Activities: books of the Old Testament and New Testament posters

Teacher Helps: Attendance Chart, Make the Most of Your Room, Some Things Should Never Change!, A Teacher's To-Do List, Leading Young Hearts Pocket Guide, Lesson Plan Outline, Transition Tips, Easels and Supports

Visuals

Sheet 3 Unit 1 Bible Memory poster, photos cards 1d–1g, photo cards for Lesson 3; Sheet 4 story figures for Lessons 1–5; Sheet 5 story figures 6a–6d, cards for Lesson 5, photo cards for Lesson 6

Weekly Bible Reader® **Issues 1–6**

Additional Activities for Unit 1

Use these activities for early arrivers, for children who finish activities quickly, and when you are waiting for parents to arrive.

"Jesus Does Great Things" Bulletin Board

Title the bulletin board "Jesus Does Great Things." Attach a picture of Jesus in the middle of the board. Print the four action labels as shown (walk on water, make people well, make people see, make people walk) and attach them on the board. Have the children draw pictures of the great things Jesus did and attach them by the labels. As children think of other great things Jesus did, let them draw those pictures and attach those on the bulletin board also.

Great Things Game

Have children sit in a circle. Tell kids to think of some of the great things Jesus did. Start by saying "Jesus did great things. He healed an official's son." Have a child next to you say "Jesus did great things. He healed an official's son, and He _____." The next child repeats what has been said and adds another great thing Jesus did. Keep going until everyone has had a turn. Help kids with ideas as needed. If kids forget what has been said, gently help them remember.

Fun Messages

Let kids make these fun messages to give to friends and family. Write or type the following and copy onto colorful paper: "It's so easy to get *hooked* on Jesus!" Remind kids of the Bible story of Jesus feeding the 5,000. Provide fish-shaped crackers in small resealable plastic bags. Have kids attach the message to each bag of fish crackers. You could also have the kids make extra bags and let them give those to family members or any guests who come to your class.

Fish Plates

Use the illustration to guide you as you trace several fish fins, tails, and heads onto poster board. Cut these out for the children to use while tracing. Have each child trace a fin, a tail, and a head from construction paper. Kids can cut out the shapes and attach them to the backs of the paper plates. They can also draw eyes and mouths. Kids could use the plates during Lesson 3, Jesus Feeds 5,000. Encourage kids to take their fish plates home and hang the plates from a ceiling or ceiling light.

Bible Skills

Make copies of the Bible Skills Worksheets for Unit 1 from the *Resources* CD. For Unit 1, children will review what a Scripture reference means.

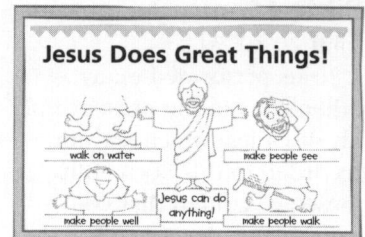

Special Note

Your students will also enjoy creating Floating Flower Surprise Messages. For craft instructions, go to www.heartshaper.com and check out the Holiday and Seasonal Helps under Teacher Resources.

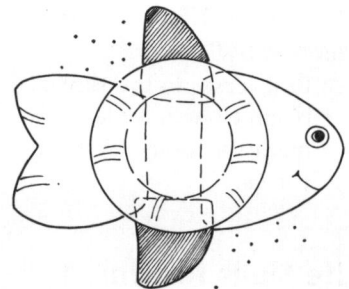

Buzzy Bee Letters

Buzzy Bee Letters, included on the *Resources* CD, provide a fun way for kids to review the weekly Bible story and life focus. Print and distribute copies. Or print one copy and post it where kids can read it. The letters can also be mailed or e-mailed to kids during the week.

Jesus Heals an Official's Son

（1）

Bible Focus: John 4:43-53
Bible Memory: Jesus performed many other signs in the presence of his disciples, which are not recorded in this book. But these are written that you may believe that Jesus is the Messiah, the Son of God (John 20:30, 31).
Life Focus: ❤ Jesus can do great things.

Heart to Heart

The children in your class can probably list several great abilities they have. But what great abilities do you have? It is true that, compared to Jesus, our abilities are small indeed. We certainly cannot heal someone with our words or touch. We cannot walk on water or raise the dead. However, in the sight of God the Father, you are doing something great when you help shape children's hearts for God. You are teaching the powerful Word of God to those Jesus holds in high esteem, His children. When you tell about the great things Jesus can do, you are doing something great yourself. You are introducing children to Jesus and His great love!

Lesson 1 at a Glance

		HeartShaper Materials	Other Materials
Step 1 **Focus In** Use one of these activities to help children *explore being sick*.	☰ *Quick Step* What Do You Need?	• *Activities* p. 9	• pencils
	Option Feeling Sick Role-Plays	• none	• real or toy medical supplies
	Bible Memory *Use this activity to introduce the Bible Memory verses.*	• none	• Bible
Step 2 **Explore His Word** Use all of these activities to help children *tell what great thing Jesus did for an official's son* and develop Bible skills.	Jesus Heals an Official's Son	• *Resources* Sheet 3 photos 1d–1g, Sheet 4 story figures 1a–1c, CD including the Review Questions printable file; *Teaching Picture* 1	• white board, dry-erase marker, Bibles, CD player
	Bible Review Activity		
	Bible Skill Builder and Bible Memory Activity		
Step 3 **Make It Real** Use one of these activities to help children *identify great things Jesus did*.	☰ *Quick Step* That's Great!	• *Activities* p. 10 and corresponding stickers	• colored pencils or crayons
	Option Great Things Game	• none	• none
	Option Story from *Weekly Bible Reader®*	• *Weekly Bible Reader®* Issue 1	• none
Step 4 **Live It Out** Use one of these activities to help children *thank Jesus for doing great things*.	☰ *Quick Step* G-R-E-A-T Cheer	• none	• none
	Option A Great Big Thank You! Saying Good-bye	• *Resources* CD	• roll paper, markers, crayons, CD player
		• *Weekly Bible Reader®* Issue 1, *Activities* p. 7 Unit 1 Bible Memory poster and stickers	• none

Focus In (15 minutes)

Step 1 • Use one of these activities to help children **explore being sick.** Use the Bible Memory activity to introduce the memory verses.

Welcome
- Welcome each child by name.
- Do check-in procedures you follow (name and security tags, offering, attendance chart, etc.).
- Early arrivers will enjoy doing one or more of the activities described on page 20.

≡ *Quick Step* What Do You Need?

Let's think about what it's like to be sick. Distribute the activity pages and pencils. Read the directions aloud and allow time for kids to do the page on their own. When all the children are done, tell kids to say "I'm sick" if they circled an item as you call it out: **a doctor's sign** (pause for kids to say "I'm sick"); **a first-aid kit** (pause for kids to say "I'm sick"); **racing cars** (no response), and so forth.

As time permits, you may want to give kids candy "pills" to play this fun bingo game. For each circled item, say something such as, **If you have ever been to the doctor's office, place a pill on that picture.** Tell kids to say "I'm sick" when they have placed five candies on their pages.

- **How do you feel when you are sick?** (yucky, fever, stomach hurts)
- **Who helps you when you are sick?** (mom, dad, grandparent, brother, sister, doctor)

The Bible tells us that ❤ Jesus can do great things. We're going to discover that He healed people who were sick.

Materials
Activities p. 9, pencils
(optional: small round candies)

Activity Page

Option   Feeling Sick Role-Plays

Let's think about what it's like to be sick. Let's use these medical supplies and do some role-plays about being sick. Show the supplies. Allow a child to choose one or two of the supplies and do a role-play about being sick. The child can choose a friend or two to help do the role-play. Give all children the opportunity to participate. Be prepared to give them some ideas as needed.

- **How do you feel when you are sick?** (yucky, fever, stomach hurts)
- **What are some things you do or someone does for you to help you feel better?** (take medicine, go to the doctor, pray, eat some soup or gelatin, stay in bed)
- **Who helps you when you are sick?** (mom, dad, grandparent, brother, sister, doctor)

The Bible tells us that ❤ Jesus can do great things. We're going to find out that He healed people who were sick.

Materials
real or toy medical supplies (bandages, stethoscope, toy syringe, toy thermometer, crutches, wheelchair, adhesive bandages)

Act It Out

Bible Memory   John 20:30, 31

Have everyone lie down (or lay their heads down) as if they are sick. Explain that you are going to read to the "sick" people to help them feel better. Read John 20:30, 31. **These are our new Bible Memory verses. According to these verses, who performed signs?** (Jesus) **Why did John write about the signs Jesus performed?** (so we would believe Jesus is the Messiah, God's Son) **Jesus can do impossible things! ❤ Jesus can do great things. He can make sick people well again. Listen closely as I read the verses again. Jump up** (or kids can raise their heads) **when I say "Messiah" to show that you believe Jesus can make sick people well.** Read the verses again.

Materials
Bible

DISCUSS

Transition to Explore His Word
See the *Resources* CD Transition Tips printable file. As children gather, make sure you have all the materials you need.

❤ Jesus can do great things.

Explore His Word (20 minutes)

Step 2 • Use all of these activities to help children **tell what great thing Jesus did for an official's son** and develop Bible skills.

Bible Background for the Teacher

Capernaum was about 20 miles from Cana or roughly a four- to five-hour walk. The royal official who asked for Jesus' help was probably a high-ranking officer in service to King Herod.

By noting that the time his son was healed was exactly when Jesus had spoken the words "Your son will live," the official understood that his son's recovery was a miracle, not a coincidence.

The official's overwhelming confidence in Jesus had an important benefit that went beyond the healing of his son. He certainly shared the details of his encounter with Jesus with his entire household, which likely included servants as well as family members. After his testimony, all of them came to believe in Jesus.

Although the people of Cana were quite excited about seeing Jesus perform miracles, this miracle was obviously not done to please or impress them, for there was nothing for those in Cana to observe. While miracles can be a wonderful sign from God (John 20:30, 31), our faith should not be dependent on them (Matthew 12:38, 39).

Worship Time

If you want to offer a time of worship, see the *Resources* CD Worship Time Ideas printable file for suggestions.

Materials

white board; dry-erase marker; Bibles; *Resources* Sheet 3 photos 1d–1g, Sheet 4 story figures 1a–1c; *Teaching Picture* 1

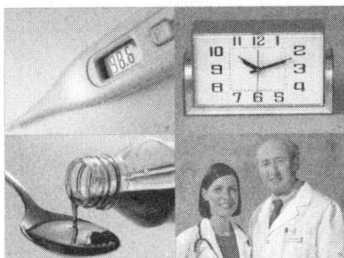

Before Class

Decide how you want to display the story figures during the story. You could attach easels, craft sticks, or paper tubes to the backs of figures. Or you may want to display them on a wall, a piece of poster board, or a bulletin board.

Jesus Heals an Official's Son (John 4:43-53)

The Bible story comes from the New Testament book of John. Write "John 4:43" on the board. Explain that *John* is a book of the Bible, *4* is the chapter number, and *43* is the verse number. Help the children turn to the book of John in their Bibles. Tell kids to then run their fingers down each column of words until they find the large number *4*. Then tell them to find the little number *43*. Ask for a volunteer to read John 4:43. Ask children to tell you who the "He" is talking about (Jesus).

Listen carefully to find out what great thing Jesus did for an official's son. And when you hear about the official's son being sick or having a fever, hold your hand over your forehead. You may want to give the story figures to children to hold during the story.

(Have your Bible open to John 4. Display the story figures and photos as indicated. Show 1a.) When Jesus came back to the town of Cana of Galilee, all the people were excited. They had seen Jesus heal sick people in Jerusalem. They remembered that He had changed water into wine at a wedding in their town. It was big news that Jesus was in town.

In the town of Capernaum lived a man who was a royal official *(1b)*. The official had a son *(1c)*. His son was very sick with a high fever *(hand on forehead; show photo 1d)*. His son was so sick that the boy was about to die.

The royal official heard that Jesus was in Cana. The official hurried to Cana to find Jesus. The official begged Jesus, "Jesus, please come back with me to Capernaum. My son is very sick *(hand on forehead)*. Please come and heal him before he dies!"

Jesus said to the official, "You can go back home. Your son is no longer sick. He will live." *(Show* Teaching Picture *1.)*

The official believed Jesus and returned home to Capernaum. On his way home, his servants met him and said, "Your son is alive. He's no longer sick *(hand on forehead)*!"

The official asked, "What time *(photo 1e)* did the boy get better?"

The servants replied, "The fever *(hand on forehead)* left your son yesterday, at one in the afternoon."

The official probably smiled. He knew that this was the exact time that he was talking with Jesus. He knew that this was the exact time that Jesus said

Life Focus
❤ Jesus can do great things.

his son would live. Then the official and the official's entire family believed in Jesus.

Jesus did not need medicine to heal the boy *(photo 1f)*. Jesus did not need doctors to heal the boy *(photo 1g)*. Jesus didn't even need to be close to the boy to make him well. He just said the words!

This was Jesus' second miracle since coming to Galilee from Judea. Jesus used His power from God to heal the official's son. The official learned that ❤ Jesus can do great things!

Bible Review Activity

What great thing did Jesus do for an official's son? (Jesus healed the official's son.) **Let's see what else you remember from the Bible story.** Give one story figure or photo to a child or pair of children. Tell the children that you will ask questions about the story. If the answer to the question is the story figure or photo they have, they should stand and hold up their figure or photo. You can use the *Resources* CD Review Questions for more questions about the story.

- **Who went to the town of Cana?** (Jesus)
- **Who begged Jesus to heal his son?** (official)
- **Who was very sick with a fever?** (boy)
- **What thing could tell how high the official's son fever was, if they would have had one back then?** (thermometer)
- **Who said, "Your son will live"?** (Jesus)
- **Who believed what Jesus said?** (official)
- **Who got better just because Jesus said he would?** (boy)
- **What thing could tell the time when the official's son got better, if they would have had one back then?** (clock)
- **What things did Jesus not need to heal the official's son?** (medicine, doctors)

❤ **Jesus can do great things. He healed people who were sick.**

Bible Skill Builder and Bible Memory Activity

Our Bible Memory verses are found in the New Testament book of John. Write "John 20:30, 31" on the board. **Find the table of contents near the front of your Bibles.** Ask kids to point to the New Testament section and then point to the book of John. Point to the Scripture reference as you talk about it. **John 20:30 and 31 are our new Bible Memory verses. *John* is the name of the book, *20* is the chapter number, and *30* and *31* are the verse numbers.** Tell the children to find the page number John begins on and turn to it. Help them find John 20:30, 31. Ask for volunteers to read the verses.

Write the words "Jesus," "book," "written," "believe," and "God" on the board. Play "John 20:30, 31" and point to the words as they are sung. Play the song again and invite kids to sing along. Let children take turns pointing to the words as they are sung. ❤ **Jesus can do great things. The Bible tells us that He performed many signs that help us believe He is God's Son. These signs were *miracles*. That means they were something only God could do.** (Note: The recorded Bible Memory song is based on the *New International Version* © 1984.).

Materials

Action

Resources Sheet 4
story figures 1a–1c,
Sheet 3 photos 1d–1g,
CD Review Questions printable file

Materials

Music

white board, dry-
erase markers, Bibles,
Resources CD Tracks 5
and 6, CD player

Added Fun!

Kids can do these motions while singing: *Jesus*—touch the middle finger of one hand to the middle of the palm of the other hand and then repeat with the other hand; *book*—the hands show a book opening; *written*—pretend to write with a finger of one hand on the palm of the other hand; *believe*—point to the head; *God*—an open hand is raised to the heavens and then downward.

Life Focus
❤ Jesus can do great things.

Make It Real (15 minutes)

Step 3 • Use one of these activities to help children **identify great things Jesus did.**

Materials
Activities p. 10 and corresponding stickers, colored pencils or crayons

Activity Page

≡≡≡ *Quick Step*   That's Great!
The Bible tells us that ❤ Jesus can do great things. He healed a boy's fever without even touching the boy or seeing him. Let's think of other great things Jesus did. Distribute the activity pages, stickers, and colored pencils or crayons. Read the directions aloud and do the page together. (Jesus rose from the tomb. *Moses* led the people across the Red Sea. Jesus healed a man who couldn't walk. Jesus calmed a storm. God gave *Moses* the Ten Commandments. Jesus healed a man who couldn't see.) After the children have drawn other great things Jesus did, have them share their pictures with the rest of the class.
• **What other great things did Jesus do?** (He died on the cross for us because He loves us. He raised people from the dead. He fed a lot of people with a little bit of food. He walked on water. He healed people.)
It's great to know that ❤ Jesus can do great things!

Materials
none

Game

Option   Great Things Game
The Bible tells us that ❤ Jesus can do great things. What are some great things Jesus did? List the children's answers on the board. (healed people, died on the cross, rose from the dead, calmed a storm, walked on water, raised people from the dead, fed a lot of people with a little bit of food)
Have kids sit or stand in a circle. Start by saying, **Jesus can do great things. He healed a man who couldn't walk.** The child next to you will repeat what you said and add one more great thing Jesus did. "Jesus can do **great things. He healed a man who couldn't walk. He fed a lot of people with a little bit of food.**" Keep going around the circle, each child adding one more great thing Jesus did. Encourage kids to not repeat what someone else has said.
❤ Jesus can do great things! He's the only one who could do all those things you named.

Materials
Weekly Bible Reader® Issue 1

LISTEN

Option   Story from *Weekly Bible Reader®*
The Bible tells us that ❤ Jesus can do great things. Let's discover some great things Jesus did. Read "How Did He Do That?"
• **What are some great things Jesus did?** (See the activities above for possible responses.)
It's great to know that ❤ Jesus can do great things!

Expert Tip
Nothing is more powerful than a passionate, enthusiastic teacher. The word *enthusiasm* is rooted in two Greek words: *en* (or "in") and *theos* (or "God"). When we're "enthusiastic" about something, we are "in God."
—*Rick Chromey*

Live It Out (10 minutes)

Step 4 • Use one of these activities to help children **thank Jesus for doing great things.**

≡ *Quick Step* G-R-E-A-T Cheer

Jesus is greater and more powerful than sickness, storms, and even death! Let's thank Jesus because ❤ Jesus can do great things. Ask children to stand. Divide the class into three groups. One group can spell the word *great* over and over. Another group can say "great, great, great" over and over. The last group can say "Jesus does great things!" over and over.

Lead children in clapping a rhythm. Do each part of the cheer separately. Then see if all groups can do their parts at the same time. (Hint: Start with the clapping and then point to the groups one by one to add their parts.)

Close with a time of prayer. Assign volunteers to thank Jesus for some of the following: dying on the cross, rising from the dead, healing people, walking on water, calming a storm, and loving us.

Option A Great Big Thank You!

❤ **Jesus can do great things. He healed sick people, like the boy with a fever in today's story. He calmed storms and walked on water. He died on the cross and rose from the dead. Let's make a big thank-You banner to thank Jesus for the great things He did!**

Before class, print outline letters that spell "Thank You, Jesus" on a long piece of roll paper. Lay the paper on a table. Assign a letter to each child or pair of children to color. Children can also sign their names on the banner. Play "Jesus Can Do Great Things" as children work. If you have pictures of Jesus doing great things, kids could put those on the banner too.

Form a prayer circle around the banner. Encourage children to pray and thank Jesus for something great He did.

Saying Good-bye

• Distribute Issue 1 of *Weekly Bible Reader®* and the *Activities* page 7 Unit 1 Bible Memory poster and stickers. Stickers are in the middle of *Early Elementary Activities.* Encourage kids to complete their posters at home by adding the stickers and coloring.

• Make sure children have projects and activity sheets they have done.

• If you have time before parents arrive, use some of the activities on page 20.

• Be sure parents know about the *Faith & Family* page available online to download and use at home. You may want to print and have a copy on display for parents to see. Go to www.heartshaper.com.

Materials
none

Materials
roll paper, markers, crayons, *Resources* CD Tracks 3 and 4, CD player
(optional: pictures of Jesus, glue)

Added Fun!
If the weather permits, this activity could be taken outside. Write the words on a sidewalk with outdoor chalk and let kids color in the letters using colored chalk.

Evaluate
• How well did the children understand that only Jesus can do the great things He did?
• How well did the activities you chose help the children learn about Jesus?

Jesus Heals a Man at a Pool

2

Bible Focus: John 5:1-9
Bible Memory: Jesus performed many other signs in the presence of his disciples, which are not recorded in this book. But these are written that you may believe that Jesus is the Messiah, the Son of God (John 20:30, 31).
Life Focus: ♥ Jesus can do miracles.

Heart to Heart

Unlike the stereotypical faith healer of today, Jesus did not make a big show of the miracles He did. In fact, many times Jesus performed miracles of healing for people who seemed to be the lowliest in that culture. The man at the pool had no one to help him—until the day Jesus helped him in a way that only Jesus could.

We can follow Jesus' example. With no fanfare or self-focus, we can humbly seek out those who seem rather lowly and/or insignificant and share with them about Jesus, the one who can do great things.

Lesson 2 at a Glance

Step			HeartShaper Materials	Other Materials
Step 1 **Focus In** Use one of these activities to help children *explore what it might be like to always stay in bed.*	*Quick Step* What Can He Do?	*Activity Page*	• *Activities* p. 11	• pencils or crayons
	Option She Needs Help	*Act It Out*	• none	• mat or blanket, props (see the activity)
	Bible Memory *Use this activity to introduce the Bible Memory verses.*	*DISCUSS*	• *Resources* CD	• Bible, CD player
Step 2 **Explore His Word** Use all of these activities to help children *tell what great thing Jesus did for a man at a pool* and develop Bible skills.	Jesus Heals a Man at a Pool	*Bible Story*	• *Resources* Sheet 3 Bible Memory poster, Sheet 4 story figures 1a, 2a, 2b, CD including the Review Questions printable file; *Teaching Picture 2*	• white board, dry-erase marker, Bibles, CD player, reusable adhesive
	Bible Review Activity	*Act It Out*		
	Bible Skill Builder and Bible Memory Activity	*Bible Skills*		
Step 3 **Make It Real** Use one of these activities to help children *identify ways to tell others that Jesus can do miracles.*	*Quick Step* Ways to Tell	*Activity Page*	• *Activities* p. 12	• pencils
	Option Pass It Quickly!	*Action*	• none	• pencil, marker, dollar bill, Bible
	Option Story from *Weekly Bible Reader®*	*LISTEN*	• *Weekly Bible Reader®* Issue 2	• none
Step 4 **Live It Out** Use one of these activities to help children *tell someone that Jesus can do miracles.*	*Quick Step* Tell Others Notebook Covers	*Art*	• reproducible p. 91	• markers, colored pencils, scissors, construction paper, glue, notebook
	Option "Jesus Can Do Great Things"	*Music*	• *Resources* CD	• CD player
	Saying Good-bye		• *Weekly Bible Reader®* Issue 2	• none

Focus In (15 minutes)

Life Focus
❤ Jesus can do miracles.

Step 1 • Use one of these activities to help children **explore what it might be like to always stay in bed.** Use the Bible Memory Activity to introduce the memory verses.

Welcome
- Welcome each child by name.
- Do check-in procedures you follow (name and security tags, offering, attendance chart, etc.).
- Early arrivers will enjoy doing one or more of the activities described on page 20.

≡ *Quick Step* What Can He Do?

Have you ever been sick and had to stay in bed? (Allow kids to share.) **There are some people who are so sick that they have to stay in bed all the time. Let's think about what it would be like to always stay in bed.**

Distribute the activity pages and pencils or crayons. Read the directions aloud. Discuss what might be wrong with the boy. Read and decide together which activities he could and could not do. Have children mark the answers on their pages. As time permits, kids could also take turns acting out other things that someone in bed can or cannot do (jump, run, watch TV, go to a restaurant). Have the rest of the class guess what is being acted out.

- **How would you feel if you always had to stay in bed?** (sad, lonely, bored)

We're going to hear today about a man who was not able to walk for many years and was not able to leave his bed.

Materials
Activities p. 11, pencils or crayons

Activity Page

Option   She Needs Help

Have you ever been so sick that you had to stay in bed? What were some things you couldn't do while you were in bed? (Allow kids to share.) Choose someone to lie on the mat or blanket. This child will pretend that she has to stay in bed. The rest of the children should help her as needed. Prompt the person in bed to ask for the following items: food, toothbrush, book, toy, TV remote, or whatever items you have. The children should not only hand her the items but also pretend to prepare the food, give her water and toothpaste along with the toothbrush, and so forth. As time permits, give all the children a turn to lie on the mat or blanket.

- **What do you think you would do if you had to stay in bed all the time?** (read, watch TV)
- **How would you feel if you always had to stay in bed?** (sad, lonely, bored)

We're going to hear today about a man who was not able to walk for many years and was not able to leave his bed.

Materials
mat or blanket, props (food item, toothbrush and paste, cup, book, TV remote, toy, etc.)

Act It Out

Bible Memory   John 20:30, 31

Read aloud John 20:30, 31 from the Bible. **In whose presence did Jesus perform many signs?** (His disciples) **Why does the Bible tell us about the many of the signs Jesus did?** (so that we may believe that Jesus is the Messiah, the Son of God) **Last week we learned that Jesus can do great things. This week we're going to learn that ❤ Jesus can do miracles.** As time permits, play "John 20:30, 31" and invite kids to sing along. Motions can be found in the Bible Skill Builder and Bible Memory Activity on page 24.

Materials
Bible, *Resources* CD Tracks 5 and 6, CD player

Discuss

Transition to Explore His Word
See the *Resources* CD Transition Tips printable file. As children gather, make sure you have all the materials you need.

Life Focus

❤ Jesus can do miracles.

Step 2 • Use all of these activities to help children **tell what great thing Jesus did for a man at a pool** and develop Bible skills.

Bible Background for the Teacher

In some manuscripts from which our Bible translations are taken, more insight is given as to why people who were disabled waited by the pool at Bethesda. The people believed that an angel of the Lord came at certain times and stirred the water. The first person to enter the water at that time would be cured. Whether this was indeed a healing mercy from God or a legend, we don't know. What we do know is that God has employed many different ways to bring about healing.

In other accounts of Jesus healing, people approached Him requesting healing for themselves or another. This man didn't seem to have any idea who Jesus was, let alone have any faith that Jesus could heal him.

Children may know people who are ill or disabled and wonder if Jesus still heals today. The Bible shares many accounts of people coming to Jesus to be healed or coming on behalf of a sick person. Today we come to Jesus through prayer. We can also lift others who are ill into Jesus' healing presence through prayer (James 5:14-16). Sometimes God chooses to heal when we ask Him. God may choose to heal through medical treatment. Or God may choose not to heal.

Worship Time

If you want to offer a time of worship, see the *Resources* CD Worship Time Ideas printable file for suggestions.

Materials

white board; dry-erase marker; Bibles; *Resources* Sheet 4 story figures 1a, 2a, 2b; *Teaching Picture* 2

Before Class

Decide how you want to display the story figures during the story. You could attach easels, craft sticks, or paper tubes to the backs of figures. Or you may want to display them on a wall, a piece of poster board, or a bulletin board.

Jesus Heals a Man at a Pool   (John 5:1-9)

The Bible story once again comes from the New Testament book of John. Write "John 5:1" on the board. Remind children that *John* is a book of the Bible, *5* is the chapter number, and *1* is the verse number. Help the children turn to the book of John in their Bibles. Tell kids to then run their fingers down each column of words until they find the large number *5*. Then tell them to find the little number *1*. Ask for a volunteer to read John 5:1.

Listen carefully to find out what great thing Jesus did for a man at a pool. When you hear me say the word *man*, I want you to say "who couldn't walk." You may want to give the story figures to children to hold during the story.

(Have your Bible open to John 5. Display the story figures as indicated. Show 1a.) Jesus went to the city of Jerusalem for a special feast. While Jesus was in Jerusalem, He visited a place called Bethesda. Bethesda was a pool of water near the temple. It was a large pool surrounded by five columns.

But Jesus was not the only one to visit Bethseda. There were many people who were sick and disabled lying by the pool. Some could not see, some could not walk easily, and some could not move their legs at all.

These people came to the pool because they believed that the first one to get into the pool after the water moved would be healed.

(Show 2a.) There was one **man** *(kids say "who couldn't walk)* lying there who had not been able to walk for 38 years. Jesus saw the **man** and learned that he had been in this condition a long time. Jesus asked the **man**, "Do you want to be well?" *(Show* Teaching Picture *2.)*

The **man** answered, "Sir, there is no one to help me get into the **pool** when the water starts moving. I try to be the first one into the water. But when I try, someone else always goes in before I can."

Jesus said to the **man**, "Get up! Pick up your mat and walk" (v. 8).

(Show 2b.) Immediately, the **man** was well! He picked up his mat and began to walk, just like Jesus told him to do. It was a miracle! Can you imagine how the **man** must have felt? After 38 years of not being able to walk, suddenly the **man** was completely well! The legs that had been too weak to get him into

the pool were now strong and healthy. It happened because ❤ Jesus can do miracles!

Bible Review Activity

What great thing did Jesus do for a man at a pool? (Jesus healed the man so he was able to walk.) Let children have fun acting out the Bible story as you retell the story. Give each child a part to act out, either as Jesus, the man who could not walk, or one of the sick people by the pool. Use the Review Questions for more questions about the story.

• **How long had the man not been able to walk?** (38 years)
• **What did Jesus tell the man to do?** (get up, pick up his mat, and walk)
• **How soon after Jesus told the man to get up was the man able to walk?** (immediately)

The man at the pool found out that day that ❤ Jesus can do miracles. And because the Bible tells us about this miracle, we can know too that ❤ Jesus can do miracles.

Materials
Resources CD Review Questions printable file
(optional: mat or blanket)

Act It Out

Bible Skill Builder and Bible Memory Activity

Write "John 20:30, 31" on the board. **Who would like to draw a box around the name of the book of the Bible?** Choose a volunteer. **Who would like to draw a triangle around the chapter number?** Choose a volunteer. **Who would like to draw a circle around the verse numbers?** Choose a volunteer. **John is the book, 20 is the chapter number, and 30 and 31 are the verse numbers.** Help children turn to John 20:30, 31 in their Bibles and ask for volunteers to read the verses.

Before class, press out the words from the bottom of the Bible Memory poster. Display the Bible Memory poster. Read the words while pointing to them. Pause when you come to an empty space and ask who knows what word is missing. When a child says the right word, let her attach that word to the poster using reusable adhesive. When all the spaces have been filled, lead the kids in saying together the memory verses.

Our Bible Memory verses tell us that Jesus performed many signs for His disciples to see. These signs were *miracles*. They were something only God could do. ❤ Jesus can do miracles. Jesus did miracles so that we can believe He is God's Son.

Materials
white board, dry-erase marker, Bibles, *Resources* Sheet 3 Bible Memory poster, reusable adhesive

Bible Skills

Teaching Tip
Print and use the Unit 1 Bible Skills Worksheets found on the *Resources* CD to help children review what a Scripture reference means.

Life Focus
❤ Jesus can do miracles.

Make It Real (15 minutes)

Step 3 • Use one of these activities to help children **identify ways to tell others that Jesus can do miracles.**

Materials
Activities p. 12,
pencils

Activity Page

≡ *Quick Step* Ways to Tell

We've learned that ❤ **Jesus can do miracles because we've heard the story about Jesus healing the man who couldn't walk. But there are many people who do not know about Jesus and His miracles. Let's think about ways that we can tell those people about Jesus' miracles.**

Distribute the activity pages and pencils. Read the directions aloud and do the page together. After following the directions, encourage children to think of specific people they can tell about Jesus' miracles. Have them write the people's names by the ways in which they will tell them.

• **What are some other ways you can tell people that ❤ Jesus can do miracles?** (read or give a Bible or a Bible storybook to a friend, send money to missionaries who tell about Jesus)

• **Who can you tell about Jesus and His miracles?** (friends, neighbors, family)

We want to tell others that ❤ **Jesus can do miracles because everyone needs to know about Jesus, the Son of God!**

Materials
pencil, marker, dollar
bill, Bible

Action

Option Pass It Quickly!

We've learned that ❤ **Jesus can do miracles. But there are many people who do not know about Jesus and His miracles. Let's think about ways we can tell those people about Jesus.** Have kids gather in a circle. Give kids a pencil and a marker and tell them to pass the items quickly around the circle. After the items have been passed around the circle, ask:

• **How could you use a pencil and/or a marker to tell that ❤ Jesus can do miracles?** (draw a picture of Jesus' miracles, make a card that tells about His miracles, write a letter and tell about Jesus' miracles)

Give kids a dollar bill and tell them to pass it quickly around the circle.

• **How could you use money to tell that ❤ Jesus can do miracles?** (buy Bibles and books about Jesus, send money to missionaries who tell about Jesus)

Give kids a Bible and tell them to pass it quickly around the circle.

• **How could you use a Bible to tell that ❤ Jesus can do miracles?** (read a Bible story to someone, give a Bible to someone)

The Bible tells us that ❤ **Jesus can do miracles. We need to tell others about Jesus and His miracles.**

Materials
Weekly Bible Reader®
Issue 2

LISTEN

Option Story from *Weekly Bible Reader*®

We've learned that ❤ **Jesus can do miracles. Let's think of some ways to tell others about Jesus and His miracles.** Read "Chantel Tells."

• **What are some ways you can tell others that ❤ Jesus can do miracles?** (See the activities above for possible responses.)

We want to tell others that ❤ **Jesus can do miracles because everyone needs to know about Jesus, the Son of God!**

Live It Out (10 minutes)

Step 4 • Use one of these activities to help children **tell someone that Jesus can do miracles.**

≡ *Quick Step* Tell Others Notebook Covers

We've learned that ❤ **Jesus can do miracles, and we've discovered ways to tell others about Jesus and His miracles. We're going to make notebook covers to help us tell others that** ❤ **Jesus can do miracles.**

Before class, make copies of reproducible page 91. Distribute the pages, markers, colored pencils, scissors, construction paper, and glue. Ask the children to describe the different miracles pictured. Children can color the pictures and then cut out the pictures and title. Let kids choose a sheet of construction paper to glue the title and pictures onto. Remind them to attach the covers to a school notebook, folder, or binder.

When kids are finished with their notebook covers, lay one of the covers on top of a notebook or book. Ask for a volunteer to hold the notebook. Pretend that you are at school and ask her about the notebook cover. **Why do you have that notebook cover? What are those pictures about? Who is Jesus? Is He the only one who could do those miracles?** Prompt the volunteer as needed to answer the questions. Give all kids the opportunity to hold the notebook and answer questions.

Close with a time of prayer. Encourage kids to pray for God's help in telling others that Jesus can do miracles.

Materials

reproducible p. 91, markers, colored pencils, scissors, construction paper, glue, notebook

Added Fun!

Provide folders for kids to put their covers on.

Option "Jesus Can Do Great Things"

We've learned that ❤ **Jesus can do miracles, and we've discovered some ways to tell others about Jesus and His miracles. Let's learn a song about the great things Jesus did that we can sing so others will know about Jesus and His miracles.**

Play "Jesus Can Do Great Things." Play again and invite the children to join in singing. Kids will enjoy doing these motions while they sing: *Jesus*—touch the middle finger of one hand to the middle of the palm of the other hand and then repeat with the other hand; *great*—with both hands open, pull the hands in slightly and then push out in an expression of wonder; *miracles*—raise both hands; *anything*—spread both arms outward.

Invite children to a closing prayer circle. Ask children to name whom they could sing the song to. Then lead the children in a time of directed prayer. Tell the children that you will give them ideas of what to pray about and then they should silently pray about each thing for a short period of time. **Start your prayer by thanking God for Jesus.** (pause for a few seconds) **Thank God that Jesus did miracles.** (pause) **Tell God the name of someone you would like to tell about Jesus and His miracles.** (pause) **Ask for God's help to tell that person about Jesus.** (pause) **In Jesus' name, amen.**

Materials

Resources CD Tracks 3 and 4, CD player

Saying Good-bye

• Distribute Issue 2 of *Weekly Bible Reader®*.

• Make sure children have projects and activity sheets they have done.

• If you have time before parents arrive, use some of the activities on page 20.

• Remind parents that a weekly *Faith & Family* page is available online to print and use with their child at home. See www.heartshaper.com.

Evaluate

• How willing were the children to tell others about Jesus and His miracles?

• How can you help children better connect with each other to form friendships?

Jesus Feeds 5,000

③

Bible Focus: John 6:1-14
Bible Memory: Jesus performed many other signs in the presence of his disciples, which are not recorded in this book. But these are written that you may believe that Jesus is the Messiah, the Son of God (John 20:30, 31).
Life Focus: ❤ Jesus can give you what you need.

Heart to Heart

What things do you need? Your physical needs include food and shelter. Your emotional needs include love and acceptance. Most importantly, your spiritual needs include the need for a Savior! Unfortunately, we tend to make the lines blurry between our needs and our wants. We begin to think we need a flat screen TV, a new car, an updated computer, the latest gadgets, and more.

Jesus gave the crowd of people the food they needed. But more importantly, Jesus came to bring people, including us, what we really need—the way to God. Thank Him for giving us what we really need.

Lesson 3 at a Glance

Step 1			HeartShaper Materials	Other Materials
Focus In Use one of these activities to help children *explore things they need.*	☰ *Quick Step* Needs vs. Wants	*Discover*	• none	• paper, marker, old magazines, store ads, catalogs, scissors, reusable adhesive
	Option What Would Happen?	*Discuss*	• none	• large sack, food items, water bottle, item of clothing, pictures (see the activity), paper heart
	Bible Memory *Use this activity to introduce the Bible Memory verses.*	*Memorize*	• *Resources* Sheet 3 Bible Memory poster	• Bible, reusable adhesive
Step 2 **Explore His Word** Use all of these activities to help children *tell what great thing Jesus did for a crowd of people* and develop Bible skills.	Jesus Feeds 5,000	*Bible Story*	• *Resources* Sheet 4 story figures 1a, 3a–3e, CD including the Review Questions printable file; *Teaching Picture* 3; *Activities* p. 14	• white board, dry-erase markers, Bibles, blanket, craft sticks, clear tape, 6 paper lunch bags, marker, pencils, CD player
	Bible Review Activity	*Activity Page*		
	Bible Skill Builder and Bible Memory Activity	*Bible Skills*		
Step 3 **Make It Real** Use one of these activities to help children *identify times to thank Jesus for giving them what they need.*	☰ *Quick Step* When I Can Thank	*Discuss*	• *Resources* Sheet 3 photo cards for Lesson 3	• none
	Option Thanking Jesus	*Activity Page*	• *Activities* p. 13	• pencils
	Option Story from *Weekly Bible Reader®*	*Listen*	• *Weekly Bible Reader®* Issue 3	• none
Step 4 **Live It Out** Use one of these activities to help children *thank Jesus for giving them what they need.*	☰ *Quick Step* Thanksgiving Walk	*Pray*	• *Resources* Sheet 3 photo cards for Lesson 3, CD	• reusable adhesive, CD player
	Option Thank-You Game	*Action*	• none	• beanbag
	Saying Good-bye		• *Weekly Bible Reader®* Issue 3	• none

Focus In (15 minutes)

Step 1 • Use one of these activities to help children **explore things they need.** Use the Bible Memory activity to introduce the memory verses.

Welcome
- Welcome each child by name.
- Do check-in procedures you follow (name and security tags, offering, attendance chart, etc.).
- Early arrivers will enjoy doing one or more of the activities described on page 20.

Quick Step   Needs vs. Wants

There are some things that each of us needs. Sometimes there are things that we *think* we need, like a television or a toy. But these are things we want, not things that we need. Let's think about things we need.

Write the words "Needs" and "Wants" on two separate sheets of paper. Display the signs on the wall or lay them on the floor with space under each sign. Let children cut out pictures of things they need (food, water, light, clothes, and so forth) and things they might want (toys, bikes, computer, and so forth). Kids should put the pictures either under the "Needs" sign or the "Wants" sign. When kids are done, point to each picture, let kids name it, and ask,

- **Can you live without water?** (no) **So water is a need.**
- **Can you live without a bike?** (yes) **So having a bike is a want, not a need.**

Do the same for each picture. **There are things that you need. We're going to learn that ❤ Jesus can give you what you need.**

Materials

paper, marker, old magazines, store ads, catalogs, scissors, reusable adhesive

Option   What Would Happen?

What are some things we need in order to live? (food, water, clothes, home, heat, way to stay cool, love) **There are items in this sack or pictures of items that we need.** Have a child pull out an item. The child should name the item and answer this question:

- **What would happen if you didn't have ____ (name of item)?** (would get very hungry, weak, sick, eventually die)

Do the same for each item in the sack. You may need to return items to the sack so each child gets a turn. **There are things that you need. We're going to learn that ❤ Jesus can give you what you need.**

Materials

large sack; food items; water bottle; item of clothing; pictures of a house, sun, tree (way to stay cool); paper heart (to represent love)

Bible Memory   John 20:30, 31

Let's read our Bible Memory verses, John 20:30 and 31. Listen for something you need to know and believe. Read aloud John 20:30, 31 from the Bible. **What do you need to know and believe?** (that Jesus is the Messiah, the Son of God) Display the Bible Memory poster. Read the words while pointing to them. Pause when you come to an empty space and ask who knows what word is missing. When a child says the right word, let him attach that word to the poster using reusable adhesive. When all the spaces have been filled, lead the kids in saying together the memory verses. **Jesus performed many signs so we would believe that Jesus is God's Son. We're going to learn that ❤ Jesus can give you what you need.**

Materials

Bible, *Resources* Sheet 3 Bible Memory poster, reusable adhesive

Transition to Explore His Word

See the *Resources* CD Transition Tips printable file. As children gather, make sure you have all the materials you need.

Life Focus

❤ Jesus can give you what you need.

Explore His Word (20 minutes)

Step 2 • Use all of these activities to help children **tell what great thing Jesus did for a crowd of people** and develop Bible skills.

Bible Background for the Teacher

This miracle of provision takes place near the time of the Passover, a feast remembering how God rescued His people from Egypt and miraculously provided for them in the desert. It is the only miracle, except the resurrection of Jesus, found in all four Gospels.

A prophet was a person who delivered messages from God to the people. Sometimes prophets validated their message was from God by performing miracles. In Luke's account of this same event, we learn that Jesus was also teaching the people who were gathered here about the kingdom of God, and He was healing those who were sick among them.

Since the 5,000 men were accompanied by women and children, the total crowd size has been estimated conservatively at 15,000 to 20,000 people. Barley was a much cheaper grain than wheat, and the loaves were not like a full loaf of bread, but more likely the size of a roll. It may be difficult for children to grasp the enormous size of this crowd compared to the small amount of food on hand. Perhaps a modern day way to picture the scope of this miracle would be to think of a major league sports stadium filled with people being fed with a few hamburgers and fries.

Worship Time

If you want to offer a time of worship, see the *Resources* CD Worship Time Ideas printable file for suggestions.

Materials

white board; dry-erase marker; Bibles; blanket; craft sticks; clear tape; 6 paper lunch bags; marker; *Resources* Sheet 4 story figures 1a, 3a–3e; *Teaching Picture* 3

Before Class

Before class, attach craft sticks to the backs of figures and put the story figures in individual lunch bags. Number the bags in the order they are used in the story.

Jesus Feeds 5,000   (John 6:1-14)

Write "John 6:1" on the board. **Our Bible story starts at this place in the Bible. Let's see if we can find this in our Bibles. *John* is the name of the book. The *6* is the chapter number. The *1* is the verse number.** Help children turn to John 6:1 in their Bibles. Have a volunteer read the verse.

Spread the blanket out for children to sit on. Hand the lunch bags to individual kids or pairs of kids. **We're going to pretend we're part of the crowd in today's story. You can help tell the story by sharing what's in your bag when I ask for your number. Everyone needs to listen for what great thing Jesus did for a crowd of people.**

(Have your Bible open to John 6. Have the child with bag #1 open it and hold up figure 1a.) One day Jesus and His friends sailed across the Sea of Galilee and a large crowd of people followed them. The people followed Jesus because they saw the miracles He did to make sick people well again. Jesus and His disciples went up on a mountainside and sat down.

When Jesus saw the large crowd, He asked Philip, one of His followers, *(bag #2, figure 3a)*, "Where can we buy bread for all these people to eat?" Now Jesus already knew how He would feed the crowd, but He asked Philip because He wanted to hear Philip's answer.

Philip said, "It would take more than half a year's salary to be able to buy enough bread for each person here to have only a little bite."

Then Andrew *(bag #3, figure 3b)*, another follower of Jesus, said, "Here is a boy *(bag #4, figure 3c)* with a lunch of five small loaves of barley bread and two small fish. But that is not enough food for so many people." *(Show Teaching Picture 3.)*

Jesus said, "Tell the people to sit down." This was a very grassy place with room for many people to sit *(bag #5, figure 3d)*. The Bible says that there were about 5,000 men. There were women and children too.

Jesus took the loaves of bread and thanked God for them. Then He gave bread to all the people. Next, Jesus took the fish, thanked God for them, and gave them to the people too. He gave the people as much as they wanted. They all had enough to eat.

When everyone was finished eating, Jesus said to His followers, "Gather the pieces that were not eaten. Do not waste anything." Jesus' followers did exactly as He said and gathered the food that was left. They filled 12 large baskets *(bag #6, figure 3e)* with the leftovers!

Just the leftovers were more food than they started with! When the people saw this miracle that Jesus did, they were amazed. They said, "Surely this is a prophet sent from God."

Bible Review Activity

What great thing did Jesus do for a crowd of people? (Jesus gave them the food they needed. Jesus fed more than 5,000 people with only five loaves of bread and two fish.) **Let's see what else you remember from the Bible story.** Distribute the activity pages and pencils. Read the directions aloud and do the page together.

As time allows, play this review game. Put all the story figures into one of the paper lunch bags. Have the children sit in a circle. Tell them to pass the bag until they hear you say "Jesus fed a crowd." Whoever is holding the bag can reach in, choose a figure, and then you can ask them a question about that figure. You can use the Review Questions for questions about the story. Make sure that all kids get to answer at least one question.

Jesus did a miracle when He gave the people the food they needed. Jesus does give us what we need. ❤ Jesus can give you what you need too.

Bible Skill Builder and Bible Memory Activity

Write "John 20:30, 31" on the board. Use a different color of marker for *John, 20,* and *30, 31*. **This Scripture reference is for our Bible Memory verses. What color is the name of the book?** (Let kids respond.) **What color is the chapter number? What color is the verse numbers? Is John in the Old or New Testament?** (New) Tell kids to find the book of John in the New Testament section in the table of contents in their Bibles. Help them turn to John 20:30, 31. Ask for volunteers to read the verses.

Play "John 20:30, 31" and encourage kids to sing along. Motions kids can do while singing can be found in the Bible Skill Builder and Bible Memory Activity on page 24.

Our Bible Memory verses tell us who Jesus is the Messiah, the Son of God. We've learned that Jesus can do great things and that Jesus can do miracles. Now we're learning that ❤ Jesus can give you what you need.

Added Fun!
Let kids enjoy pieces of bread and fish-shaped crackers during or after the story.

Materials
Activities p. 14; pencils; paper lunch bag; *Resources* Sheet 4 story figures 1a, 3a–3e, and CD Review Questions printable file

Activity Page

Materials
white board, 3 different colors of dry-erase markers, Bibles, *Resources* CD Tracks 5 and 6, CD player

Bible Skills

Expert Tip
"Ministry to children is about effecting change in the lives of the children who then have a powerful influence in the home.

—*Steve Alley*

Life Focus

❤ Jesus can give you what you need.

Make It Real (15 minutes)

Step 3 • Use one of these activities to help children **identify times to thank Jesus for giving them what they need.**

Materials
Resources Sheet 3 photo cards for Lesson 3

DISCUSS

Added Fun!
Play a game. Say, **I can thank Jesus for bananas when I'm hungry.** The child next to you says "I can thank Jesus for bananas and ___ when I'm hungry." Keep going around the circle, each child adding one more food item.

Quick Step   When I Can Thank

Jesus gave more than 5,000 people the food they needed, and ❤ Jesus can give you what you need too. What are some things Jesus gives us that we need? (food, water, family, love, Bible, home, friends) **Let's think of times we can thank Jesus for giving us what we need.**

Give the photo cards to six individual children, pairs, or small groups of children. Two photos show kids at school. Ask the kids holding those photos to answer this question, letting the photos help them with answers:

• **For what can you thank Jesus when you're at school?** (a place to learn, water, teachers, friends, books, recess)

Three photos show kids at home. Ask the kids holding those photos to answer this question:

• **For what can you thank Jesus when you're at home?** (family, food, water, home, love, bed, safety, clothes, Bible, being cared for, brothers and sisters, pets)

One photo shows kids outside. Ask the child holding this photo to answer this question:

• **For what can you thank Jesus when you're outside?** (friends, sun, having fun, bikes, trees, flowers)

It's great to know that ❤ Jesus can give you what you need. Remember to thank Him!

Materials
Activities p. 13, pencils

Activity Page

Option   Thanking Jesus

Jesus gave more than 5,000 people the food they needed, and ❤ Jesus can give you what you need too. What are some things Jesus gives us that we need? (food, water, family, love, Bible, home, friends) **Let's think of times we can thank Jesus for giving us what we need.** Distribute the activity pages and pencils. Read the directions aloud and do the page together.

• **When are some other times you can thank Jesus for giving you what you need?** (I can thank Him for teachers and the Bible while at Sunday school. I can thank Him for food while at a restaurant or grocery store. I can thank Him for teachers and books while at school. I can thank Him for sun and trees while I'm outside.)

It's great to know that ❤ Jesus can give you what you need. There are lots of times each day that you can thank Him.

Materials
Weekly Bible Reader® Issue 3

LISTEN

Option   Story from *Weekly Bible Reader*®

Jesus gave more than 5,000 people the food they needed, and ❤ Jesus can give you what you need too. Let's think of times we can thank Jesus for giving us what we need. Read "Rachel's Day."

• **When are some times you can thank Jesus for giving you what you need?** (See the activities above for possible responses.)

It's great to know that ❤ Jesus can give you what you need. Remember to thank Him!

Live It Out (10 minutes)

Step 4 • Use one of these activities to help children **thank Jesus for giving them what they need.**

≡ *Quick Step* **Thanksgiving Walk**

Jesus does great things! He gave more than 5,000 people the food they needed. And we know that ♥ Jesus can give you what you need. Let's thank Jesus now for giving us what we need. Let's thank Jesus now for giving us what we need.

Display the photo cards in different areas of your room. Lead the class in walking as a group, stopping at each photo, and forming a prayer circle. Ask for volunteers to say prayers at each photo, thanking Jesus for giving us the things pictured in the photo. The prayers could be something like this: **Thank You, Jesus, for giving us a home and a bed. Thank You, Jesus, for giving us a family, the Bible, love, and brothers and sisters.**

As time permits after the thanksgiving walk, play and sing "Jesus Can Do Great Things." Motions can be found in the Step 4 Option Activity on page 32.

Materials
Resources Sheet 3 photo cards for Lesson 3, CD Tracks 3 and 4; reusable adhesive; CD player

Pray

Option Thank-You Game

Jesus does great things! He gave more than 5,000 people the food they needed. And we know that ♥ Jesus can give you what you need. Let's thank Jesus now for giving us what we need. Have the children sit or stand in a circle. Tell the kids that you will toss the beanbag to one of them and that child should say "Thank You, Jesus, for giving me ___," naming something he needs that Jesus has given him. That child should toss the beanbag back to you and you then toss it to another child. Continue until everyone has had at least one turn to thank Jesus.

Close with a time of prayer. Invite children to thank Jesus for giving them what they need.

Materials
beanbag

Action

Saying Good-bye
• Distribute Issue 3 of *Weekly Bible Reader*®.
• Make sure children have projects and activity sheets they have done.
• If you have time before parents arrive, use some of the activities on page 20.
• Remind parents that a weekly *Faith & Family* page is available online to print and use with their child at home. See www.heartshaper.com.

Evaluate
• How did the children demonstrate they understood that Jesus gives them what they need?
• Did you give all children the opportunity to ask and answer questions?

Jesus Walks on Water

Bible Focus: Matthew 14:22-33
Bible Memory: Jesus performed many other signs in the presence of his disciples, which are not recorded in this book. But these are written that you may believe that Jesus is the Messiah, the Son of God (John 20:30, 31).
Life Focus: ❤ Jesus can do anything.

Heart to Heart

Have you heard the phrase, "You can do anything you set your mind to"? It is true that we can accomplish big things if we depend on God's help and work hard. However, it is not true that we can do anything. None of us can walk on water. None of us can multiply fish and bread. None of us can heal the sick with our words. Certainly none of us can raise the dead! But the Son of God really can do anything! What an awesome motivation to bow before the Savior in humble worship. What an awesome motivation to teach children to bow before their Savior in humble worship!

Lesson 4 at a Glance

		HeartShaper Materials	Other Materials
Step 1 **Focus In** Use one of these activities to help children *explore* *water.*	**Quick Step** What's Wet?	• reproducible p. 92	• pencils
	Option Water Laboratory	• none	• plastic tub, water, towel, items that will float or sink
	Bible Memory *Use this activity to introduce the Bible Memory verses.*	• reproducible p. 93	• scissors, craft sticks, clear tape, Bible
Step 2 **Explore His Word** Use all of these activities to help children *tell what great things Jesus did on a lake* and develop Bible skills.	Jesus Walks on Water	• *Resources* Sheet 4 story figures 1a, 4a, 4b, Sheet 3 Bible Memory poster, CD; *Teaching Picture* 4	• white board, dry-erase markers, Bibles, reusable adhesive, CD player,
	Bible Review Activity		
	Bible Skill Builder and Bible Memory Activity		
Step 3 **Make It Real** Use one of these activities to help children *discover ways to worship Jesus.*	**Quick Step** I Can Worship Jesus	• *Activities* p. 15 and corresponding stickers	• scissors, clear tape or glue
	Option Worship Game	• none	• none
	Option Story from *Weekly Bible Reader®*	• *Weekly Bible Reader®* Issue 4	• none
Step 4 **Live It Out** Use one of these activities to help children *worship Jesus; He can do anything.*	**Quick Step** Worshiping Jesus	• *Activities* p. 15	• none
	Option "Jesus Can Do Great Things"	• *Resources* CD	• CD player
	Saying Good-bye	• *Weekly Bible Reader®* Issue 4	• none

Focus In (15 minutes)

Step 1 • Use one of these activities to help children **explore water.**
Use the Bible Memory activity to introduce the memory verses.

Welcome
- Welcome each child by name.
- Do check-in procedures you follow (name and security tags, offering, attendance chart, etc.).
- Early arrivers will enjoy doing one or more of the activities described on page 20.

≡≡≡ *Quick Step* What's Wet?

What are some things you like to do in water? (Let children share.)
**Everyone needs and uses water every day for all kinds of things. Let's
see what we know about water as we solve some fun riddles.** Before class,
make copies of the reproducible page. Distribute the pages and pencils. Read
the directions aloud and do the page together.
- **What are some things people use water for?** (wash clothes and dishes
in it, drink it, take a bath in it, take a boat out on it)
- **What can you do with water when it's frozen?** (ice skate, make ice
cubes, maybe walk on it)
- **What would happen if you tried to walk on water if it wasn't frozen?**
(sink)
**Today's Bible story has to do with water. We're going to find out that
♥ Jesus can do anything.**

Materials
reproducible p. 92,
pencils

Activity Page

Option Water Laboratory

What are some things you like to do in water? (Let children share.) **Let's
pretend we are scientists investigating water. Let's find out what floats
and what doesn't.** Set out the tub of water with a towel underneath. One
at a time, give an item to a child to put in the tub. Before doing so, let the
child guess whether the item will float or sink. Be sure that each child has the
opportunity to place her hands on the surface of the water and press down.
- **Why do you think some things float and some sink?** (some are heavy,
some have a lot of air in them)
- **Can people float in water?** (yes) **Can people float if they stood up and
tried to float?** (no)
**Today's Bible story has to do with water. We're going to find out that
♥ Jesus can do anything.**

Materials
plastic tub or bucket
filled with water, towel,
items that will float or
sink (rock, leaf, paper
clip, pencil, paper cup, coin)

Discover

Bible Memory John 20:30, 31

Before class, make a copy of the reproducible page (you may want to
enlarge the signs). Cut out the signs and attach craft sticks to the backs. Read
aloud John 20:30, 31. **What does our Bible Memory verses say Jesus did?**
(performed many signs) **What kind of signs are these verses talking about?**
(miracles) **The Bible says that Jesus made a boy's fever stop.** Hold up the
stop sign. **Jesus told a man who could not walk, to get up and go, and
he did.** Hold up the go sign. **Jesus made storms yield to Him.** Hold up the
yield sign. **Jesus is the *only* one who can do these miraculous signs.** Hold
up the one-way sign. **Jesus is God's Son. ♥ Jesus can do anything!**

Materials
reproducible p. 93,
scissors, craft sticks,
clear tape, Bible

DISCUSS

Transition to Explore His Word
See the *Resources* CD Transition Tips
printable file. As children gather,
make sure you have all the materials
you need.

Life Focus

♥ Jesus can do anything.

Step 2 • Use all of these activities to help children **tell what great things Jesus did on a lake** and develop Bible skills.

Bible Background for the Teacher

The boat that the disciples were in was out in the middle of the Sea of Galilee when the storm became severe. The disciples really were in danger.

At first, the disciples did not recognize Jesus. It was only when they heard His voice that they knew it was Jesus. Some children may have been taught "there is no such thing as ghosts." This passage may create confusion then, since the disciples of Jesus seemed to believe in the possibility of their existence. The disciples may have simply been influenced by the superstitions of their day, desperately trying to make sense of something they saw (someone walking on water) but did not understand.

It is unclear how far Peter was able to walk on the water. Jesus told Peter he had only a little faith, yet Peter was the only one who stepped out of the boat and walked on water.

Several miracles occurred: Jesus walked on water; Peter walked on water; and the wind died down when Jesus got into the boat. The disciples responded to these miracles by worshiping Jesus. This is the first time the disciples called Jesus the Son of God.

Worship Time

If you want to offer a time of worship, see the *Resources* CD Worship Time Ideas printable file for suggestions.

Materials

white board; dry-erase markers; Bibles; *Resources* Sheet 4 story figures 1a, 4a, 4b, CD Track 10; reusable adhesive; CD player; *Teaching Picture* 4

Jesus Walks on Water   (Matthew 14:22-33)

Write "Matthew 14:22" on the board. **Our Bible story is in Matthew 14. Let's find this in our Bibles.** Point to each part as you explain it. **We need to find the book of Matthew. It is the first book in the New Testament. Then we need to find chapter 14 and verse 22.** Make sure each child is successful in finding the Scripture. Ask for a volunteer to read the verse.

Our Bible story takes place by a lake and a mountain. On the board, draw a lake with a mountain beside it. **You're going to pretend you are with Jesus' followers in a boat. You're going to act out what they might have done and say what they said. And you need to listen for a great thing Jesus did on a lake.**

(Have your Bible open to Matthew 14. Using adhesive, display the story figures on the white board as indicated.) After Jesus fed more than 5,000 people using only five loaves of bread and two fish, He dismissed the people so they could return to their homes. Jesus then told His followers to get into the boat and go to the other side of the Sea of Galilee. *(Attach 4a on the lake, close to the mountain.)* Jesus went up on a mountainside to be alone and to pray to God. *(Attach 1a on the mountain.)*

When it was evening, the boat was a long way from the shore. *(Move the boat further from the mountain.)* The wind started to blow and the waves started to get big. *(Play the storm sound effects. Continue playing it while you talk.)* The wind blew stronger and stronger. The followers of Jesus were working hard to keep their boat afloat in the dangerous waves. *(Kids can sway and pretend to hold onto the sides of a boat.)*

During the night, Jesus went out to meet His followers. *(Move 1a toward 4a.)* He walked on the water to get to them! *(Show Teaching Picture 4.)* His followers saw Jesus walking on the water, and they were terrified. They cried out in fear, "It's a ghost!" *(Kids look afraid and repeat "It's a ghost!")*

Immediately Jesus spoke to them. He said, "Take courage! It is I. Don't be afraid" (v. 27).

Peter cried out to Jesus, "Jesus, if that's You, let me come to You."

Jesus said, "Come."

(Put 4b on the water close to 1a.) Peter got out of the boat and walked

Life Focus
♥ Jesus can do anything.

toward Jesus. He was walking on the water too. But when Peter looked around and heard the wind, he became afraid and started to sink. Peter cried out to Jesus, "Lord, save me!"

Jesus immediately reached out His hand and caught Peter. Jesus asked Peter, "Why did you doubt? You have only a little bit of faith."

(Remove 1a and 4b.) After Jesus and Peter climbed into the boat, the wind died down. *(Stop the storm sound effects. Kids can look amazed.)* The followers in the boat worshiped Jesus and said, "Truly you are the Son of God." (v. 33; *Kids repeat "Truly you are the Son of God."*)

Bible Review Activity

What great things did Jesus do on a lake? (He walked on water. He saved Peter from sinking. He made the wind die down.) **Let's see what else you remember from the story.**

If Jesus told His followers to get into a boat, pretend to row a boat. (pretend to row)

If Jesus went up a mountainside to go get hamburgers and fries, say "yummy, yummy." (no)

If Jesus wanted to be alone to pray to God, fold your hands in prayer. (fold hands)

If the followers' boat was a long way from shore when the wind started, make a noise like the wind. (blow like the wind)

If the followers went to sleep in the boat, pretend to sleep. (no)

If Jesus walked on the water to get to the boat, pretend to walk on water. (walk on water)

If Jesus' followers thought He was a ghost, look afraid. (look afraid)

If Tommy wanted to go to Jesus, say "I want to come." (no)

If Jesus caught Peter when he started to sink, raise an arm. (raise arms)

If the followers of Jesus worshiped Jesus, bow your head. (bow heads)

Once again, Jesus did a miracle and showed He is God's Son. And this miracle further shows us that ♥ Jesus can do anything!

Materials
none

Action

Bible Skill Builder and Bible Memory Activity

Write "John 20:30, 31" on the board. **This Scripture reference is for our Bible Memory verses. Who can underline and tell us the name of the book?** (John) **Who can circle and tell us the chapter number?** (20) **Who can put a check mark by and tell us the numbers of the verses?** (30, 31). Tell kids to turn to the table of contents in their Bibles and find the New Testament book of John. They should run their fingers down the page until they find John. Help children turn to the book of John. **Run your fingers down each column of words until you find the large number 20. Now find the little numbers 30 and 31.** Ask for volunteers to read the verses.

Display the Bible Memory poster. Read the words while pointing to them. Pause when you come to an empty space and ask who knows what word is missing. When a child says the right word, let her attach that word to the poster using reusable adhesive. When all the spaces have been filled, lead the kids in saying together the memory verses. **Jesus is God's Son. Jesus performed many signs that were miracles. ♥ Jesus can do anything!**

Materials
white board, dry-erase marker, Bibles, *Resources* Sheet 3 Bible Memory poster, reusable adhesive

Memorize

Teaching Tip
Print and use the Unit 1 Bible Skills Worksheets found on the *Resources* CD to help children review what a Scripture reference means.

Life Focus
❤ Jesus can do anything.

Make It Real (15 minutes)

Step 3 • Use one of these activities to help children **discover ways to worship Jesus.**

Materials
Activities p. 15 and corresponding stickers, scissors, clear tape or glue

Activity Page

≡ *Quick Step* I Can Worship Jesus

We've heard about the great things Jesus did on a lake. The followers of Jesus worshiped Jesus after they saw Him walk on the water. Let's think about ways we can worship Jesus. *Worship* means "telling Jesus how special He is." Distribute the activity pages, stickers, scissors, clear tape or glue. Read the directions aloud. Let kids add the stickers where they choose. Help kids as needed to cut out and assemble the shapes. The shape is a pyramid.

• **How can you worship Jesus with your mouth?** (pray to Him, sing a song to worship Him, tell Him He's special)
• **How can you worship Jesus with your feet?** (go and tell others about Him, go to a church service to worship Him)
• **How can you worship Jesus with your heart?** (love Him, love others)
• **How can you worship Jesus with your hands?** (fold hands to pray, draw a picture to worship Jesus, serve others, give money to Him)

There are many ways to worship Jesus. We want to worship Jesus because ❤ Jesus can do anything!

Materials
none

Game

Added Fun!
Vary the kind and size of steps kids take. Let kids call out ways to worship/not worship Jesus.

Option   Worship Game

We've heard about the great things Jesus did on a lake. The followers of Jesus worshiped Jesus after they saw Him walk on the water. Let's think about ways we can worship Jesus. *Worship* means "telling Jesus how special He is." Have kids line up across the room from you to play a game. Read each sentence below. If a sentence describes a way to worship Jesus, kids should move toward you by taking one medium-size step. If they move toward you and a sentence does not describe a way to worship Jesus, have them take one step backward.

We can worship Jesus by singing praise songs to Him. (yes) We can worship Jesus by telling Him He's special. (yes) We can worship Jesus by reading a comic book. (no) We can worship Jesus by telling others about Him. (yes) We can worship Jesus by praying to Him. (yes) We can worship Jesus by talking when the teacher is talking. (no) We can worship Jesus by loving Him. (yes) We can worship Jesus by serving others. (yes) We can worship Jesus by reading the Bible. (yes)

There are many ways to worship Jesus. We want to worship Jesus because ❤ Jesus can do anything!

Materials
Weekly Bible Reader® Issue 4

LISTEN

Option   Story from *Weekly Bible Reader®*

We've heard about the great things Jesus did on a lake. The followers of Jesus worshiped Jesus after they saw Him walk on the water. Let's think about ways we can worship Jesus. *Worship* means "telling Jesus how special He is." Read "Cody and Friends."

• **What are some ways to worship Jesus?** (See the activities above for possible responses.)

We want to worship Jesus because ❤ Jesus can do anything!

Live It Out (10 minutes)

Step 4 • Use one of these activities to help children **worship Jesus; He can do anything.**

═══ *Quick Step* Worshiping Jesus

We want to worship Jesus because Jesus does great things. In fact, ❤ **Jesus can do anything!** Ask the children to hold their completed pyramids made in Step 3. If you did not have the kids do this activity in Step 3, have them do it now. **Look at your worship pyramids and think of the many ways to worship Jesus. Decide how you want to worship Jesus this week.** Ask for volunteers to share how they plan to worship Jesus.

Close with a time of prayer. **Let's worship Jesus right now by praying to Him.** Ask kids to repeat the following prayer sentences after you. **Dear Jesus, we want to worship You.** (pause; kids repeat) **We worship You because You can do great things.** (pause; kids repeat) **We worship You because You can do miracles.** (pause; kids repeat) **We worship You because You can give us what we need.** (pause; kids repeat) **We worship You because You can do anything.** (pause; kids repeat) **We worship You because You are special.** (pause; kids repeat) **We worship You because You love us.** (pause; kids repeat) **In the name of Jesus, amen.**

Materials
worship pyramids from Step 3 (*Activities* p. 15)

Option "Jesus Can Do Great Things"

We want to worship Jesus because Jesus does great things. In fact, ❤ **Jesus can do anything! Let's worship Jesus by singing a song to Him that tells about some of the great things He has done.** Play "Jesus Can Do Great Things" and encourage children to join in singing. Motions can be found in the Step 4 Option Activity on page 32.

Close with a prayer circle. Remind the children that praying is another great way to worship Jesus. Ask for volunteers to worship Jesus by praying the following sentence prayers, along with anything else they desire to pray:
1. We worship You, Jesus, because You can do great things. 2. We worship You, Jesus, because You can do miracles. 3. We worship You, Jesus, because You can give us what we need. 4. We worship You, Jesus, because You can do anything. 5. We worship You, Jesus, because You are special. 6. We worship You, Jesus, because You love us.

Materials
Resources CD Tracks 3 and 4, CD player

Saying Good-bye
• Distribute Issue 4 of *Weekly Bible Reader*®.
• Make sure children have projects and activity sheets they have done.
• If you have time before parents arrive, use some of the activities on page 20.
• Remind parents that a weekly *Faith & Family* page is available online to print and use with their child at home. See www.heartshaper.com.

Evaluate
• In what ways did the children show they know what it means to worship Jesus?
• What actions do you need to take to help children better obey the classroom rules?

Jesus Brings a Young Man Back to Life

Bible Focus: Luke 7:11-17
Bible Memory: Jesus performed many other signs in the presence of his disciples, which are not recorded in this book. But these are written that you may believe that Jesus is the Messiah, the Son of God (John 20:30, 31).
Life Focus: ❤ Jesus can make people live again.

Heart to Heart

Most of us have had to walk "through the darkest valley" (Psalm 23:4) at some point in our lives. If you have not faced the death of a close friend or family member, or stared down death yourself, no doubt you will. For Christians, though, death is not the end. We know that there is light! And that light is Jesus who has proven His power over death. He provides the hope and confidence we need to face the valley again and again. How important it is to share this hope and light with the children you teach.

Lesson 5 at a Glance

			Heartshaper Materials	Other Materials
Step 1 **Focus In** Use one of these activities to help children *explore what makes people happy and sad.*	≡ *Quick Step* Happy and Sad	Action	• *Resources* Sheet 5 cards for Lesson 5	• none
	Option Happy and Sad Faces	Action	• none	• paper plates, markers
	Bible Memory *Use this activity to introduce the Bible Memory verses.*	DISCUSS	• *Resources* Sheet 3 Bible Memory poster	• Bible, reusable adhesive
Step 2 **Explore His Word** Use all of these activities to help children *tell what great thing Jesus did for a mother* and develop Bible skills.	Jesus Brings a Young Man Back to Life	Bible Story	• *Resources* Sheet 4 story figures 1a, 5a–5d, CD including the Review Questions printable file; *Teaching Picture 5*	• white board, dry-erase marker, Bibles, paper plate faces made in Step 1, CD player
	Bible Review Activity	DISCUSS		
	Bible Skill Builder and Bible Memory Activity	Memorize		
Step 3 **Make It Real** Use one of these activities to help children *discover ways to praise Jesus.*	≡ *Quick Step* Name Ways to Praise	Action	• none	• none
	Option Praise Jesus!	Craft	• *Activities* p. 17	• markers or colored pencils; scissors; clear tape or glue; hole punch, yarn, and crepe streamer for windsocks or construction paper for posters
	Option Story from *Weekly Bible Reader®*	LISTEN	• *Weekly Bible Reader®* Issue 5	• none
Step 4 **Live It Out** Use one of these activities to help children *praise Jesus; He can make people live again.*	≡ *Quick Step* Windsock Praise	Action	• *Resources* CD	• windsocks or posters made in Step 3, CD player
	Option Praise Cheer Saying Good-bye	Sign Language	• none	• none
			• *Weekly Bible Reader®* Issue 5	• none

Focus In (15 minutes)

Step 1 • Use one of these activities to help children explore **what makes people happy and sad.** Use the Bible Memory activity to introduce the memory verses.

Welcome
- Welcome each child by name.
- Do check-in procedures you follow (name and security tags, offering, attendance chart, etc.).
- Early arrivers will enjoy doing one or more of the activities described on page 20.

Quick Step Happy and Sad

Raise your hand if you've ever been happy. Raise your hand if you've ever been sad. Let's think about what makes people happy and sad. One at a time, show the cards. Ask for a volunteer to describe what's happening in the picture. Tell kids that if what is pictured on a card would make them happy, they should clap their hands or give someone a high five. Tell kids to use their hands to cover their faces if what is pictured on a card would make them sad.
- **What are some other things that might make you happy?**
- **What are some other things that might make you sad?**

There are lots of things that make us either happy or sad. In today's Bible story we're going to hear about someone who was sad, but later became happy.

Materials
Resources Sheet 5 cards for Lesson 5

Action

Option Happy and Sad Faces

What makes you happy? What makes you sad? (Let children respond.) Distribute the supplies. Have children draw a happy face on one side of the paper plate and a sad face on the other side. Tell kids that you will name a situation. If the situation makes them happy, they should hold up the happy face side. If it makes them sad, they should hold up the sad face side.

You got a puppy. Your sister ate the last cookie. Your grandma brought you a toy. Your cousins came to visit. You are sick. It is sunny outside. It is raining. You are having spinach for dinner. You got a good grade on a test. Your friend is spending the night. Someone you know died. You get to have a friend over to your home. Someone said something mean to you. Your family is going to the movies.

There are lots of things that make us either happy or sad. In today's Bible story we're going to hear about someone who was sad, but later became happy.

Materials
paper plates, markers

Action

Added Fun!
Let kids name situations that make people happy and sad.

Bible Memory John 20:30, 31

Read aloud John 20:30, 31 from the Bible. **The many signs Jesus performed were miracles. Where did Jesus do these miracles?** (in the presence of His disciples) **Why are Jesus' miraculous signs written about in the Bible?** (so we can believe He is the Messiah, God's Son) Display the Bible Memory poster. Read the words while pointing to them. Pause when you come to an empty space and ask who knows what word is missing. When a child says the right word, let him attach that word to the poster using reusable adhesive. When all the spaces have been filled, lead the kids in saying together the memory verses. **We've been learning that Jesus can do great things. Today we're going to hear that ❤ Jesus can make people live again!**

Materials
Bible, *Resources* Sheet 3 Bible Memory poster, reusable adhesive

DISCUSS

Transition to Explore His Word
See the *Resources* CD Transition Tips printable file. As children gather, make sure you have all the materials you need.

Life Focus
♥ Jesus can make people live again.

Step 2 • Use all of these activities to help children **tell what great thing Jesus did for a mother** and develop Bible skills.

Bible Background for the Teacher

Nain was a town not far from Jesus' hometown of Nazareth. On the day Jesus visited Nain and raised the dead man to life, Jesus was enjoying a period of popularity and much activity.

Jesus had compassion for the woman. Without a husband or a son, she would probably become destitute, unable in that society to earn a living. Jesus did not tell the mother to not cry because it was wrong to cry. It's fine to cry when one is sad. But Jesus knew the miracle He was about to do and that the mother would no longer need to cry.

A large crowd of mourners followed the grieving mother. Family members customarily buried the dead outside the city shortly after death had occurred. In accordance with Jewish custom, the dead man's body was placed on a *bier*. Unlike today's closed coffins, the bier was most likely an open hand-barrow used for carrying dead bodies. Jesus restored the man to a healthy life. A very sad occasion turned to one of joy!

Jesus also raised a little girl from the dead (Mark 5) as well as His friend Lazarus (John 11). These were the only people recorded in Scripture whom Jesus raised from death while He was on the earth. Each of them later died again.

Worship Time
If you want to offer a time of worship, see the *Resources* CD Worship Time Ideas printable file for suggestions.

Materials
white board; dry-erase marker; Bibles; paper plate faces made in Step 1; *Resources* Sheet 4 story figures 1a, 5a–5d; *Teaching Picture* 5

Bible Story

Before Class
Decide how you want to display the story figures during the story. You could attach easels, craft sticks, or paper tubes to the backs of figures. Or you may want to display them on a wall, a piece of poster board, or a bulletin board.

Jesus Brings a Young Man Back to Life   (Luke 7:11-17)

Write "Luke 7:11" on the board. **The Bible is divided into two main parts, the Old Testament and the New Testament. Which part tells about Jesus' miracles?** (New Testament) **Let's find the book of Luke in the New Testament. Then we need to find the big number 7, which is the chapter number. Then we need to find the small 11, which is the verse number.** Help children turn to Luke 7:11 and ask for a volunteer to read the verse.

If the children did not make happy and sad paper plate faces in the Step 1 Option Activity, have them do it now. **When you hear about something sad in the Bible story, show the sad face. When you hear about something happy, show the happy face. You also need to listen for a great thing Jesus did for a mother.** Prompt the children as needed to show the happy and sad paper plate faces.

(Have your Bible open to Luke 7. Display the story figures as indicated.) One day Jesus *(1a)* traveled to the town of Nain. A large crowd of people, including His followers, was traveling with Him. Just as Jesus and His friends came to the town gate, they saw a crowd of people coming out of the town. It was a funeral *(sad faces)*.

A dead person was being carried out of the town. Then Jesus saw a woman crying *(5a; sad faces)*. This woman's son had died. Her husband had already died *(sad faces)* and now her son was dead too. Her friends walked with her to bury her son *(5b)*. It was a sad day *(sad faces)*.

Jesus cared that the mother was sad. Jesus said to the mother, "Don't cry."

Then Jesus went up to the bier and touched it. The men carrying the bier stopped. Jesus said to the young man on the bier, "I tell you to get up!"

(Show Teaching Picture 5.*)* The man who had been dead sat up *(5c; happy faces)*! The man began to talk. He was alive! Jesus gave the young man back to his mother *(happy faces)*.

Everyone was amazed! They had never seen anything like this before. They began praising God. They said, "A great prophet has come to us! God is taking care of His people" *(happy faces)*.

Explore His Word (continued)

News about Jesus making the young man live again spread to all the towns around. People learned that Jesus can make people live again *(happy faces)*!

Bible Review Activity

What great thing did Jesus do for a mother? (He made her son alive again.) **Let's use our happy and sad paper plate faces to see what else you remember from the Bible story.** Tell the kids to listen to the following questions. They should answer the questions by holding up either the happy face or the sad face. You can use the Review Questions for more questions about the story.

- **How did the mother feel at the beginning of the story?** (sad)
- **How did the crowd of people with the mother feel at the beginning of the story?** (sad)
- **How did Jesus feel when He saw the mother?** (sad)
- **How did the mother feel after Jesus made her son live again?** (happy)
- **How did the crowd feel when they saw the mother's son live again?** (happy)
- **How do you think the young man who was brought back to life might have felt?** (happy)

Jesus did another miracle. This miracle, like the others, shows us that Jesus does great things, including the fact that ❤ Jesus can make people live again.

Bible Skill Builder and Bible Memory Activity

Who remembers the Scripture reference for our Bible Memory verses? (John 20:30, 31) **Who can write the name of the book?** (Let a volunteer write "John" on the board.) **Who can write the chapter number? Who can write the verse numbers?** Lead the children in saying the Scripture reference together. Then help children turn to John 20:30, 31 in their Bibles. Ask for volunteers to read the verses.

Play "John 20:30, 31" and invite children to sing along. Ask kids to sit in a circle. Play the song again while kids pass the teaching picture around the circle. When the music stops, the child holding the teaching picture can lead the rest of the class in saying the Bible Memory verses together. Play as time permits.

It's great to know that ❤ Jesus can make people live again. The miracles, or "many signs," Jesus performed are written in the Bible so we can know Jesus is the Messiah, the Son of God.

Story Option
Play the recorded Bible story from the *Resources* CD Track 12.

Materials
paper plate faces made in Step 1, *Resources* CD Review Questions printable file

DISCUSS

Materials
white board, dry-erase marker, Bibles, *Resources* CD Tracks 5 and 6, CD player, *Teaching Picture* 5

Memorize

Expert Tip
"We want children to develop a heart for others, live a life of service, and love others as themselves."

—*Jody Capehart*

Life Focus

❤ Jesus can make people live again.

Make It Real (15 minutes)

Step 3 • Use one of these activities to help children **discover ways to praise Jesus.**

Materials

Added Fun!

Instead of naming ways to praise Jesus, let kids act out ways to praise Him.

Materials

Activities p. 17; markers or colored pencils; scissors; clear tape or glue; hole punch, yarn, crepe streamer for windsocks or construction paper for posters

Materials

Weekly Bible Reader® Issue 5

≡ *Quick Step*   Name Ways to Praise

The people praised God when they saw that ❤ **Jesus can make people live again. Let's discover ways we can praise Jesus.** Tell the children that you are going to point to different body parts. When they know a way to use that body part to praise Jesus, they should stand. Call on one of the children to name a way to praise Jesus, using that body part.

1. mouth (sing praise songs, tell Jesus He's special, pray to Him) 2. eyes (read the Bible) 3. ears (listen to Scriptures and Bible stories) 4. hands (serve others, put money in offering basket, draw a picture that praises Him) 5. feet (tell others about Him, serve others, go to a church service to praise Him)

We want to praise Jesus because of the great things He does and because ❤ Jesus can make people live again.

Option   Praise Jesus!

The people praised God when they saw that ❤ **Jesus can make people live again. Let's discover ways we can praise Jesus.** Distribute the activity pages, markers or colored pencils, and scissors. Read the directions aloud. Ask kids to name the ways to praise Jesus which are pictured on the activity page.

• **What are some other ways to praise Jesus?** (love Him, tell Him He's special, go to a church service to praise Him, give money to Him, draw a picture that praises Him)

Kids should draw in the empty box another way to praise Jesus and decorate the page. Then have kids cut on the cutting lines. You can have kids either make a windsock or a poster.

Windsock: Help kids roll the page lengthwise, overlap the ends a little, and tape or glue together. Kids can punch two holes at the top of the windsocks and attach yarn to form handles. Kids can attach crepe paper streamers to the bottom.

Poster: Kids can glue or tape the cut out page on a sheet of construction paper and decorate as they choose.

This windsock (or poster) can remind you of ways to praise Jesus. Remember, we can praise Jesus because ❤ Jesus can make people live again.

Option   Story from *Weekly Bible Reader®*

The people praised God when they saw that ❤ **Jesus can make people live again. Let's discover ways we can praise Jesus.** Read "Now You're Praising!"

• **What are some ways to praise Jesus?** (See the activities above for possible responses.)

We want to praise Jesus because of the great things He does and because ❤ Jesus can make people live again.

Live It Out (10 minutes)

Step 4 • Use one of these activities to help children **praise Jesus; He can make people live again.**

Quick Step   Windsock Praise

It makes us sad when people die. But we can be happy because ♥ Jesus can make people live again! Let's be happy and praise Jesus together! Show kids how to hold their windsocks up high so the streamers flow behind them. If you did not have kids make the windsocks in Step 3, let kids make them now. Have the children walk around the room with their windsocks as you play "Jesus Can Do Great Things." If you had kids make posters in Step 3, kids can hold up their posters while singing "Jesus Can Do Great Things."

Close with a time of prayer. Encourage all children to pray and praise Jesus.

Materials
windsocks or posters made in Step 3 (*Activities* p. 17), *Resources* CD Tracks 3 and 4, CD player

Action

Option   Praise Cheer

It makes us sad when people die. But we can be happy because ♥ Jesus can make people live again! Let's be happy and praise Jesus together with a cheer! Tell the children that they will say "We praise You, Jesus!" after each sentence you say about Jesus. Gather in a circle. Say the following sentences and encourage children to give their praises to Jesus. Kids may enjoy starting very softly and gradually getting louder as they repeat "We praise You, Jesus!" Kids will enjoy doing these motions while they do the cheer: *praise*—the forefinger is upright and moves straightforward from the mouth and then clap hands; *Jesus*—touch the middle finger of one hand to the middle of the palm of the other hand and then repeat with the other hand.

Jesus, You are the Son of God. (Kids say "We praise You, Jesus!")
Jesus, You do great things! (Kids say "We praise You, Jesus!")
Jesus, You did miracles. (Kids say "We praise You, Jesus!")
Jesus, You can give us what we need. (Kids say "We praise You, Jesus!")
Jesus, You can do anything. (Kids say "We praise You, Jesus!")
Jesus, You can make people live again. (Kids say "We praise You, Jesus!")
We praise You, Jesus! (Kids say "We praise You, Jesus!")
Close with a time of prayer.

Materials
none

Sign Language

Saying Good-bye

• Distribute Issue 5 of *Weekly Bible Reader*®.
• Make sure children have projects and activity sheets they have done.
• If you have time before parents arrive, use some of the activities on page 20.
• Remind parents that a weekly *Faith & Family* page is available online to print and use with their child at home. See www.heartshaper.com.

Evaluate
• How eager were children to praise Jesus?
• How well prepared were you for the class session? What should you do differently next week?

Jesus Heals Jairus's Daughter

6

Bible Focus: Mark 5:21-24, 35-42

Bible Memory: Jesus performed many other signs in the presence of his disciples, which are not recorded in this book. But these are written that you may believe that Jesus is the Messiah, the Son of God (John 20:30, 31).

Life Focus: ❤ Jesus can do great things.

Heart to Heart

The word *great* has several meanings and is used to describe numerous things. In referring to Jesus and His miracles as "great," we are referring to nearly every meaning Webster's dictionary gives for the word. The things Jesus has done and continues to do are "extremely large in quantity." They are "extensive and remarkable in magnitude, degree, and extent." They are "superior, powerful, influential, and of outstanding importance and significance." Anything else that we try to describe with all of these phrases just does not measure up. Each time you and the children you teach use the word *great*, remember to worship Jesus, the only one who truly fits the descriptions of the word!

Lesson 6 at a Glance

		HeartShaper Materials	Other Materials
Step 1 **Focus In** Use one of these activities to help children *explore what people think are great things.*	*Quick Step* If You Think It's Great **Option** What's Great? **Bible Memory** *Use this activity to introduce the Bible Memory verses.*	• *Resources* Sheet 5 photo cards for Lesson 6 • reproducible p. 94 • *Resources* Sheet 3 Bible Memory poster	• white board, dry-erase marker • pencils • reusable adhesive
Step 2 **Explore His Word** Use all of these activities to help children *tell what great thing Jesus did for Jairus* and develop Bible skills.	Jesus Heals Jairus's Daughter **Bible Review Activity** **Bible Skill Builder and Bible Memory Activity**	• *Resources* Sheet 4 story figure 1a, Sheet 5 story figures 6a–6d, CD including the Review Questions printable file; *Teaching Picture* 6	• paper, marker, craft sticks, clear tape or glue, white board, dry-erase marker, Bibles, CD player
Step 3 **Make It Real** Use one of these activities to help children *list reasons to worship Jesus.*	*Quick Step* Why Worship Jesus? **Option** Worship Signs **Option** Story from *Weekly Bible Reader®*	• *Activities* p. 19 • reproducible p. 93 • *Weekly Bible Reader®* Issue 6	• pencils, scissors, construction paper, glue, markers, decorating supplies (see p. 55) • markers, scissors, craft sticks, clear tape • none
Step 4 **Live It Out** Use one of these activities to help children *worship Jesus; He can do great things.*	*Quick Step* Worshiping Jesus **Option** "Jesus Can Do Great Things" Saying Good-bye	• none • *Resources* CD • *Weekly Bible Reader®* Issue 6	• worship posters made in Step 3 • CD player • none

Focus In (15 minutes)

Step 1 • Use one of these activities to help children **explore what people think are great things.** Use the Bible Memory activity to introduce the memory verses.

Welcome
- Welcome each child by name.
- Do check-in procedures you follow (name and security tags, offering, attendance chart, etc.).
- Early arrivers will enjoy doing one or more of the activities described on page 20.

≡ *Quick Step*   If You Think It's Great

We say that lots of things are great. When we say that candy is great, we mean that it tastes good. When we say that a toy is great, we mean we really like it. Let's think about what people think are great things. Before this activity, write the following words on the white board: elephant, White House, soccer, money, sports car, and awards. Show kids the photo card of the White House.

If you think the White House, where the president lives, is a great thing, give a big salute. Count the number of hands and put that number by the name "White House" written on the board. **If you think that elephants are great, swing your arms like an elephant's trunk.** Put that number by the name "elephant." Do the same for the other photos: awards—clap hands; money—pretend to count money; soccer—kick a leg; sports car—say "Wow!"

• **What are some other things people think are great?**

There are a lot of things we may think are great, but we know that only ❤ Jesus can do great things!

Materials
white board, dry-erase marker, *Resources* Sheet 5 photo cards for Lesson 6

Action

Option   What's Great?

We say that lots of things are great. When we say that candy is great, we mean that it tastes good. When we say that a toy is great, we mean we really like it. Let's think about what people think are great things. Before class, make copies of the reproducible page. Distribute the pages and pencils. Read the directions aloud and let kids work on the page on their own. When the children are done, name each item, asking kids to raise their hands when you name something they circled.

• **What are some other things people think are great?**
• **What other things do you think are great?**

There are a lot of things we may think are great, but we know that only ❤ Jesus can do great things!

Materials
reproducible p. 94, pencils

Activity Page

Bible Memory   John 20:30, 31

Display the Bible Memory poster. **Join me in saying our Bible Memory verses.** After kids have said the verses with you, divide the class into two groups. Have one group say the first sentence and the other group the second sentence. Then have the groups say their verses three times, starting softly and getting a little louder each time. **These verses tell us a lot about Jesus: He performed many signs, or miracles. He is the Messiah and He is the Son of God. Today we're going to keep learning that ❤ Jesus can do great things!**

Materials
Resources Sheet 3 Bible Memory poster, reusable adhesive

DISCUSS

Transition to Explore His Word
See the *Resources* CD Transition Tips printable file. As children gather, make sure you have all the materials you need.

Life Focus

❤ Jesus can do great things.

Explore His Word (20 minutes)

Step 2 • Use all of these activities to help children **tell what great thing Jesus did for Jairus** and develop Bible skills.

Bible Background for the Teacher

A synagogue ruler would have been in charge of administrative responsibilities at the synagogue, the building where people worshiped. They would have arranged for services and looked after the building. Jairus obviously had heard about Jesus' power and believed that Jesus could heal his daughter.

Jesus chose to take only three of His followers—Peter, James, and John—to the home of Jairus. These men seemed to be especially close to Jesus. It was customary for a family to hire professional mourners, people who would wail and mourn at the time of death of a family member.

Perhaps it was these professional mourners who so quickly stopped crying to laugh at Jesus when He said that the girl was only sleeping. They knew the little girl was dead. What they didn't know was that Jesus is the one who created life. To Jesus, her death was no more serious than a nap.

Jesus didn't allow any of the mourners, except the girl's mother and father, to witness the raising of the little girl. Jesus likely didn't want the news that He could raise people from the dead to spread to His enemies at this time. He was not yet finished preaching about the kingdom of Heaven.

Worship Time

If you want to offer a time of worship, see the *Resources* CD Worship Time Ideas printable file for suggestions.

Materials

white board; dry-erase marker; Bibles; paper; marker; craft sticks; clear tape or glue; *Resources* Sheet 4 story figure 1a, Sheet 5 story figures 6a–6d; *Teaching Picture* 6

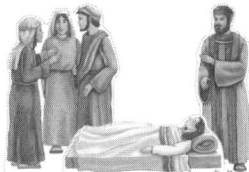

Before Class

Make two location signs and display them in different areas in your room: Sea of Galilee and Home of Jairus. Attach craft sticks to the backs of figures.

Jesus Heals Jairus's Daughter (Mark 5:21-24, 35-42)

The Bible story comes from the book of Mark. Write "Mark 5:21" on the board. **Is the book of Mark in the Old Testament or New Testament?** (New) Tell the children to look at the Scripture reference on the board. **On the count of three, everyone say the name of the Bible book. 1, 2, 3!** (Mark) **On the count of two, everyone say the chapter number. 1, 2!** (5) **On the count of one, everyone say the verse number. 1!** (21) **Now you need to find Mark 5:21 in your Bibles.** Help children turn to Mark 5:21 in their Bibles. Ask for a volunteer to read the verse.

Since today's Bible story takes place in two different places, let's pretend to travel with Jesus and His followers to these two places. And you need to listen for what great thing Jesus did for a man named Jairus (Jye-rus).

(Have your Bible open to Mark 5. Show the story figures as indicated. Show 1a.) Jesus did a lot of teaching by a very large lake called the Sea of Galilee. *(Have the class travel with you to stand by the Sea of Galilee sign.)* One time Jesus and His followers sailed in a boat from one side of the lake to the other side. When they reached the other side, a large crowd of people gathered around Jesus. They probably wanted to hear what Jesus would say and hoped to see Jesus make sick people well.

A man named Jairus *(6a)* came to Jesus. Jairus was a ruler at the synagogue, a building where Jewish people worshiped. Jairus fell down at the feet of Jesus and pleaded, "I have a 12-year-old daughter. She is dying. Please, please come with me. Please heal her so she will not die."

But while Jesus was still speaking to someone in the crowd, some men came from Jairus's house. They said, "Jairus, your daughter is dead. Don't bother Jesus anymore."

Jesus ignored the message and said to Jairus, "Don't be afraid. You just need to believe in me."

Jesus took Peter, James, and John with Him to Jairus's house. *(Have the class travel with you to stand by the Home of Jairus sign.)* At Jairus's house, people were crying loudly because the little girl was dead *(6b)*.

Jesus asked, "Why are you crying? The girl is not dead. She's only sleeping."

The people stopped crying and started laughing. They probably thought, *"This man doesn't know what He's talking about. The girl is dead."*

Jesus ignored the laughing and asked the people to leave. Jesus took His three followers and the girl's mother and father into the room where the girl was *(6c)*.

Jesus held the girl's hand and said to her, "Little girl, I tell you to get up." The girl stood right up *(6d)* and began walking. Everyone was amazed! *(Show Teaching Picture 6.)*

Bible Review Activity

What great thing did Jesus do for Jairus? (Jesus brought Jairus's daughter back to life.) **Let's act out this exciting story!** Assign as many parts as possible: Jesus, Jairus, Jairus's daughter, Jairus's wife, men from Jairus's house, Peter, James, John, and the crowd. Encourage children to act out their parts as you play the recorded Bible story. Provide Bible-times costumes if possible. When finished acting out the story, you may want to use the Review Questions to ask children questions about the story.

Jairus, his wife, and the people at his house learned that ♥ Jesus can do great things! Jesus is greater than anyone else. He has power even greater than death!

Bible Skill Builder and Bible Memory Activity

Write "John 20:30, 31" on the board. Tell the children to look at the Scripture reference on the board. **On the count of three, everyone say the name of the Bible book. 1, 2, 3!** (John) **On the count of two, everyone say the chapter number. 1, 2!** (20) **On the count of one, everyone say the verse numbers. 1!** (30, 31) **Now you need to find John 20:30, 31 in your Bibles.** Remind children how to find the verses and help them as needed to turn to John 20:30, 31. Ask for volunteers to read the verses.

Play "John 20:30, 31" and encourage kids to sing along. Motions kids can do while singing can be found in the Bible Skill Builder and Bible Memory Activity on page 24. Ask who would like to say the verses from memory. Encourage all the kids to try.

Only Jesus, the Son of God, could do the great things Jesus did—healing people, feeding a large crowd of people with only a little bit of food, walking on water, and making people live again. ♥ Jesus can do great things!

Story Option
Play the recorded Bible story from the *Resources* CD Track 13.

Materials
Resources CD Track 13 and the Review Question printable file, CD player (optional: Bible-times costumes)

Act It Out

Materials
white board, dry-erase marker, Bibles, *Resources* CD Tracks 5 and 6, CD player

Memorize

Life Focus

❤ Jesus can do great things.

Make It Real (15 minutes)

Step 3 • Use one of these activities to help children **list reasons to worship Jesus.**

Materials

Activities p. 19, pencils, scissors, construction paper, glue, markers, decorating supplies (glitter glue, stickers, etc.)

Activity Page

Added Fun!

Let kids act out reasons we should worship Jesus while the rest of the class guesses what they are doing.

Materials

reproducible p. 93, markers, scissors, craft sticks, clear tape

DISCUSS

Teaching Tip

Copying the signs onto card stock will make them sturdier for children to use.

Added Fun!

Play a game. Divide the class into two groups. Have the groups stand together and face you. Hold up the *go* sign. Ask each group to name something that Jesus made to *go*. The groups can take two steps toward you for each correct answer. Do the same with the other signs.

Materials

Weekly Bible Reader® Issue 6

LISTEN

☰☰ *Quick Step*   Why Worship Jesus?

Everyone was amazed when Jesus made the daughter of Jairus live again. They found out that ❤ Jesus can do great things. Let's think of reasons why we want to worship Jesus, the one who can do great things. Distribute the activity pages and supplies. Read the directions aloud and do the page together.

In the first section, both words start with *a* (awesome, anything). In the second section, both words start with *m* (miracles, mighty). In the third section, both words start with *w* (walked, with). In the fourth section, both words start with *h* (healed, helps). Have kids cut on the cutting lines. Then have kids glue the cutout onto construction paper to make special worship posters. They can color and decorate the posters as they desire.

• **Do you know other reasons we should worship Jesus?** (He's God's Son. He brought people back to life. He died on the cross for us. He rose from the dead. He loves us.)

It's important that we worship ❤ Jesus, the one who can do great things!

Option   Worship Signs

Jairus, his family, and all the people found out that ❤ Jesus can do great things. Let's think of reasons why we want to worship Jesus, the one who can do great things. Before class, make copies of the reproducible page. Distribute the pages and supplies. Have kids cut out the signs and attach craft sticks to the backs.

Let's think about the great things we know Jesus did. When I mention a great thing Jesus did, hold up the *go* sign if I'm describing something Jesus made to go. Hold up the *stop* sign if I'm describing something Jesus stopped. Hold up the *yield* sign if I'm describing something that yielded to Jesus. Hold up the *one-way* sign if I'm describing something only Jesus could do.

Jesus healed a boy from his fever. (stop sign, one way sign) **Jesus healed a man's legs.** (go sign, one way sign) **Jesus fed over 5,000 people.** (one way sign) **Jesus walked on water.** (yield sign, one way sign) **Jesus brought a young man back to life.** (one way sign) **Jesus made the wind die down.** (yield sign, one way sign) **Jesus brought Jairus's daughter back to life.** (one way sign)

• **What are some other reasons to worship Jesus?** (He can do anything. He died for us. He loves us.)

These are all reasons to worship Jesus. We want to worship ❤ Jesus, the one who can do great things!

Option   Story from *Weekly Bible Reader*®

Everyone was amazed when Jesus made the daughter of Jairus live again. They found out that ❤ Jesus can do great things. Let's think of reasons why we want to worship Jesus, the one who can do great things. Read "A Sick Friend."

• **What are some reasons to worship Jesus?** (See the activities above for possible responses.)

It's important that we worship ❤ Jesus, the one who can do great things!

Live It Out (10 minutes)

Step 4 • Use one of these activities to help children **worship Jesus; He can do great things.**

═ Quick Step Worshiping Jesus

Materials
worship posters made in Step 3 (*Activities* p. 19)

We know that ❤ **Jesus can do great things! He can do miracles. He can give us what we need. He can make people live again. He can do anything! These are all reasons to worship Jesus. Let's worship Jesus now.**

Have kids bring their worship posters to a closing time of prayer. If you did not have kids make the worship posters in the *Quick Step* activity in Step 3, have kids make them now.

Look at your worship posters. We learned that Jesus is awesome and can do anything. Bow your heads and silently worship Jesus because He is awesome and can do anything. Pause for a few moments. **Look at your posters again. We learned that Jesus did miracles and Jesus is mighty. Bow your heads and silently worship Jesus because He did miracles and is mighty.** Pause for a few moments. **Look at your posters again. We learned that Jesus walked on water and that Jesus is always with us. Bow your heads and silently worship Jesus because He walked on water and is always with us.** Pause for a few moments. **Look at the last section on your posters. We learned that Jesus healed people and that Jesus helps us. Bow your heads and silently worship Jesus because He healed people and He helps us.** Pause for a few moments and then close with prayer.

Option "Jesus Can Do Great Things"

Materials
Resources CD Tracks 3 and 4, CD player

We know that ❤ **Jesus can do great things! He can do miracles. He can give us what we need. He can make people live again. He can do anything! These are all reasons to worship Jesus. Let's worship Jesus by singing a song to Him that tells about some of the great things He has done.** Play "Jesus Can Do Great Things" and encourage children to join in singing. Motions can be found in the Step 4 Option Activity on page 32.

Close with a time of prayer. Tell the children that you will give them prayer thoughts and then they will use those thoughts to pray silently to worship Jesus. **Tell Jesus that you want to worship Him.** (pause for a few moments) **Tell Jesus how special He is.** (pause) **Thank Jesus that He can do great things.** (pause) **Thank Jesus that He can do anything.** (pause) **Thank Jesus that He is God's Son.** (pause) **Tell Jesus that you want to worship Him.** (pause) **In Jesus' name, amen.**

Saying Good-bye

Evaluate
• How did the children demonstrate that they understand what it means to worship Jesus?
• How well did the activities you chose help the children learn about the importance of worshiping Jesus?

• Distribute Issue 6 of *Weekly Bible Reader*®. Also hand out the *Activities* page 7 Unit 1 Bible Memory poster and stickers and the Mystery Ink™ pages if you have not already done so.
• Make sure children have projects and activity sheets they have done.
• If you have time before parents arrive, use some of the activities on page 20.
• Remind parents that a weekly *Faith & Family* page is available online to print and use with their child at home. See www.heartshaper.com.

Unit 2

	Bible Focus	Life Focus
Lesson 7 Peter Preaches About Jesus	The Day of Pentecost. Acts 1, 2	♥ We can follow Jesus.
Lesson 8 Peter and John at the Temple	Peter heals a man who can't walk. Acts 3	♥ We can tell others about Jesus.
Lesson 9 Peter and John Speak Boldly	Peter and John speak before the religious leaders. Acts 4	♥ We can speak boldly about Jesus.
Lesson 10 Philip Teaches a Man from Ethiopia	Philip and the man from Ethiopia. Acts 8	♥ We can understand God's Word.
Lesson 11 Peter and Tabitha	Peter raises Tabitha from the dead. Acts 9	♥ We can believe in Jesus.

Bible Memory

Acts 4:19, 20

But Peter and John replied, "Which is right in God's eyes: to listen to you, or to him? You be the judges! As for us, we cannot help speaking about what we have seen and heard."

Print the Additional Bible Memory file from the Resources CD for more Bible Memory verses kids will enjoy learning.

Bible Skill for Unit 2

Children will

* name the first five books of the New Testament.

Ongoing Bible Skills

Children will

* find verses in the Bible.
* begin to read Bible verses.
* memorize selected Bible verses.

Life Skills for Unit 2

Children will

* desire to follow Jesus.
* tell others about Jesus.
* plan ways to better understand God's Word.

HeartShaper Materials for Unit 2

Early Elementary Activities, **Lessons 7–11 and the Unit 2 Bible Memory Poster and Stickers**
Early Elementary Teaching Pictures, **Lessons 7–11**
Early Elementary Resources
CD
"Silver and Gold Have I None," Tracks 7, 8
"Judge for Yourselves," Track 11
Bible Story for Lesson 10, Track 14
Bible Memory: Additional Bible Memory for Unit 2 (*NIV* and *KJV*),
Bible Memory for Unit 2 (*NIV* and *KJV*)
Bible Skills Worksheets, Unit 2
Buzzy Bee Letters, Lessons 7–11
Worship Time Ideas, Unit 2
Review Questions, Unit 2
Letter to Families, Unit 2
Posters and Activities: "Judge for Yourselves" rhythm activity (words provided in both *NIV* and *KJV*), books of the Old Testament posters, books of the New Testament posters
Teacher Helps: Attendance Chart, Leading Young Hearts Pocket Guide, Lesson Plan Outline, Make the Most of Your Room, Some Things Should Never Change!, A Teacher's To-Do List, Transition Tips, Easels and Supports
Visuals
Sheet 4 story figures 1a, 5b; Sheet 5 story figure 6b, picture cards for Lesson 7; Sheet 6 Bible Memory poster, Peter and John headpieces; Sheet 7 game board, pictures 10a and 10b, picture cards; Sheet 8 story figure 7a, name cards, picture cards 8a, 9a, 9b, 11a, bulletin board title card and cards
Weekly Bible Reader® **Issues 7–11**

Additional Activities for Unit 2

Use these activities for early arrivers, for children who finish activities quickly, and when you are waiting for parents to arrive.

"The Church Teaches" Bulletin Board

Title the bulletin board "The Church Teaches." If you have access to a picture of your church building, enlarge it and put it in the center of the bulletin board. If not, draw a picture of a church building and put it on the bulletin board. Let kids color the church building. Put the following phrases on separate pieces of colorful paper: follow Jesus, tell about Jesus, speak boldly about Jesus, know God's Word, and believe in Jesus. Let the kids put these on the board also.

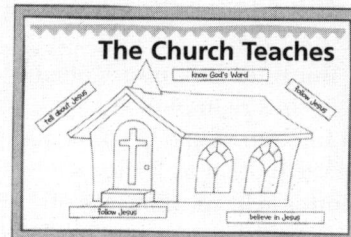

Sew a Treat

This craft could be used as a Mother's Day gift kids could give their moms, or it can remind the children of the story of Tabitha. Cut matching hearts from colorful poster board and clear, stiff plastic (such as is used on report covers). Make one set per child. The hearts should be 5½"–6" across. Punch holes around both hearts to form a sewing card. Tie on a 2' length of yarn at the top of the heart. Wrap a small piece of tape around the other end of the yarn to form a needle. Give each child a set of hearts with yarn. Show the children how to sew around the hearts, lacing them together. When the heart is almost sewn closed, let kids insert several wrapped pieces of candy inside the pocket. Sew the heart completely closed, tying a bow at the end. Encourage the children to give their treats to their moms, or others they want to tell about Jesus.

Tic-Tac-Toe Review Game

Using masking tape, make a large tic-tac-toe grid on the floor. Divide the class into two teams. Give each team several sheets of the same color of construction paper. Alternate asking the teams questions. When a team answers a question correctly, a child from that team can hold a sheet of construction paper and stand in one of the grids. Keep playing until a team gets three in a row. Questions for each Bible story can be found on the *Resources* CD Review Questions printable file.

Praying Hands Chain

Fold each sheet of construction paper in half lengthwise and cut into two strips. Fold each strip in half and then two more times to form accordion folds. Use the pattern as a guide to cut out the shape of a hand from the folded paper. Make a chain of four hands for each child.

Have the children draw pictures of people they want to ask for God's help in speaking boldly to about Jesus. Or they could draw pictures of people for whom they desire to pray. Display the praying hands chain in your classroom.

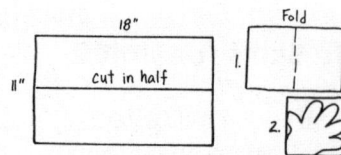

Bible Skills

Make copies of the Bible Skills Worksheets for Unit 2 from the *Resources* CD. For Unit 2, children will name the first five books of the New Testament.

Buzzy Bee Letters

Don't forget to print and distribute the weekly Buzzy Bee letters, included on the *Resources* CD. The letters can be used as discussion starters when you have extra moments at the end of class time. Students who are absent from class will look forward to receiving the letters too!

Peter Preaches About Jesus

(7)

Bible Focus: Acts 1:1-14; 2:1-8, 14, 22-24, 36-42
Bible Memory: But Peter and John replied, "Which is right in God's eyes: to listen to you, or to him? You be the judges! As for us, we cannot help speaking about what we have seen and heard" (Acts 4:19, 20).
Life Focus: ❤ We can follow Jesus.

Heart to Heart

There seems to be lots of people who think they are worth following. The movie star who makes millions may think she is worth following. But what is worth following—the temporary fame she has enjoyed? The sports celebrity who has received awards may think he is worth following. But what is worth following—his bragging and showng off?

But don't worry—there is someone who is worth following. The one who was born in a manger. The one who did miracles. The one who died for us. The one who rose from the dead. The one who loves us. Jesus—He's the one worth following.

Lesson 7 at a Glance

		HeartShaper Materials	Other Materials
Step 1 **Focus In** Use one of these activities to help children *explore what the* church *is.*	**Quick Step** What Is the Church? *(Discover)*	• *Activities* p. 21	• pencils, Bibles
	Option What Does the Church Look Like? *(Art)*	• none	• paper, markers
	Bible Memory *Use this activity to introduce the Bible Memory verses.* *(Discuss)*	• none	• Bible
Step 2 **Explore His Word** Use all of these activities to help children *describe the first time Peter told a crowd about following Jesus* and develop Bible skills.	Peter Preaches About Jesus *(Bible Story)* **Bible Review Activity** *(Action)* **Bible Skill Builder and Bible Memory Activity** *(Bible Skills)*	• *Resources* Sheet 4 story figures 1a and 5b, Sheet 5 story figure 6b, Sheet 6 Peter's headpiece, Sheet 8 story figure 7a, CD including the Review Questions and "Judge for Yourselves" printable files; *Teaching Picture* 7	• white board, dry-erase marker, Bibles, clear tape, CD player
Step 3 **Make It Real** Use one of these activities to help children *identify times to follow Jesus.*	**Quick Step** Following Jesus *(Activity Page)*	• *Activities* p. 22	• colored pencils or markers
	Option Times to Follow *(Act It Out)*	• *Resources* Sheet 5 picture cards for Lesson 7	• none
	Option Story from *Weekly Bible Reader* *(Listen)*	• *Weekly Bible Reader®* Issue 7	• none
Step 4 **Live It Out** Use one of these activities to help children *choose a time they will follow Jesus.*	**Quick Step** What We Can Do *(Art)*	• *Resources* Sheet 8 title card and card for Lesson 7	• pushpins or reusable adhesive, construction paper, crayons, markers, scissors
	Option Time to Follow Game *(Game)*	• *Teaching Picture* 7	• none
	Saying Good-bye	• *Weekly Bible Reader®* Issue 7, *Activities* p. 31 Unit 2 Bible Memory poster and stickers	• none

Focus In (15 minutes)

Life Focus

❤ We can follow Jesus.

Step 1 • Use one of these activities to help children **explore what the church is.**
Use the Bible Memory activity to introduce the memory verses.

Welcome
- Welcome each child by name.
- Do check-in procedures you follow (name and security tags, offering, attendance chart, etc.).
- Early arrivers will enjoy doing one or more of the activities described on page 58.

≡ *Quick Step*   What Is the Church?

Let's explore what the church is. Distribute the activity pages, pencils, and Bibles. Divide the class into four pairs or small groups. Read the directions aloud. Assign each pair or small group one of the Scriptures to look up and write the missing words on the blank lines.

When all the groups are done, have a child from the first group read aloud Psalm 100:2. Have another child read the first sentence with the missing word filled in. Have another child do the same with the second sentence. Then ask the other groups to fill in the missing words on their pages. Do the same with the other three groups.
- **What are some things the church does?** (worships, loves, prays, shares)
- **Who does these things?** (the church, people who love and follow Jesus)
- **What/who is the church?** (A group of people who come together to worship God. They believe in Jesus and follow Him.)

Since we are the church, we believe in Jesus and ❤ we can follow Jesus too.

Materials
Activities p. 21, pencils, Bibles

Teaching Tip
Pair advanced readers with those less advanced.

Option   What Does the Church Look Like?

Today we're going to think about the church. I'm going to give you some paper and markers. I want you to draw what you think the church is, what the church looks like, and what the church does.

Distribute the supplies. Without saying much more, allow children to draw. When everyone has finished, let children share what they drew. Without being critical of what the children have drawn, talk about the fact that, even though we may call the building where we worship and learn about God the church building, the church is really the people.
- **What are some things the church does?** (serves, loves, prays, shares, worships God, sings, follows Jesus, tells others about Jesus)
- **What/who is the church?** (A group of people who come together to worship God. They believe in Jesus and follow Him.)

Since we are the church, we believe in Jesus and ❤ we can follow Jesus too.

Materials
paper, markers

Bible Memory   Acts 4:19, 20

Raise your hand if you are supposed to obey your parents. Ask a few kids to name ways they obey their parents. **Raise your hand if you are supposed to obey your teachers.** Ask a few kids to name ways they obey their teachers. **Raise your hand if you are supposed to obey a coach.** Ask a few kids to name ways they obey their coaches. **Raise your hand if you are supposed to obey God.** Read aloud Acts 4:19, 20. **Peter and John knew that they needed to obey God, no matter what. We need to obey God too. We obey God when we follow Jesus.**

Materials
Bible

Transition to Explore His Word
See the *Resources* CD Transition Tips printable file. As children gather, make sure you have all the materials you need.

Life Focus
❤ We can follow Jesus.

Explore His Word (20 minutes)

Step 2 • Use all of these activities to help children **describe the first time Peter told a crowd about following Jesus** and develop Bible skills.

Bible Background for the Teacher
Pentecost was a Jewish feast held 50 days after the Sabbath of the Passover week. At Pentecost, the Jews remembered when the law was first given to Israel. Today, the church remembers Pentecost as when the Holy Spirit was first given to followers of Jesus.

Wind or *breath* is often used as a symbol for the Spirit of God. The coming of the Holy Spirit was marked with both visible and audible signs (fire and wind). Further evidence of the coming of the Holy Spirit was that the followers of Jesus could speak in languages they had never studied. These languages were real languages. People from all over the world could now hear about Jesus in their own native languages. While all the followers of Jesus could speak in different languages, Peter served as the spokesman.

The question with which the audience responded (Acts 2:37) showed that they believed Peter and that they felt great remorse for what they had done to Jesus. The word *repent* means more than saying "I am sorry." *Repent* means to change. Two promises are given to those who repent and are baptized: forgiveness of sins and the gift of the Holy Spirit.

Worship Time
If you want to offer a time of worship, see the *Resources* CD Worship Time Ideas printable file for suggestions.

Materials
white board; dry-erase marker; Bibles; *Resources* Sheet 4 story figures 1a and 5b, Sheet 5 story figure 6b, Sheet 6 Peter's headpiece, Sheet 8 story figure 7a; *Teaching Picture* 7; clear tape

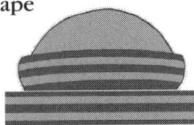

Before Class
Put together Peter's headpiece as described on Sheet 6. Decide how you want to display the story figures during the story. You could attach easels, craft sticks, or paper tubes to the backs of figures. Or you may want to display them on a wall, a piece of poster board, or a bulletin board.

Peter Preaches About Jesus (Acts 1:1-14; 2:1-8, 14, 22-24, 36-42)
Our Bible story comes from the book of Acts. Write "Acts 2:1" on the board. **Acts is in the New Testament.** Have the children turn to the table of contents in the front of their Bibles. They should look in the New Testament section and run their fingers down until they find Acts. Help children turn to Acts 2:1 and ask for a volunteer to read the verse.

Choose a child to wear Peter's headpiece and act out what Peter does. **You all can help tell today's Bible story. When you hear a number, count it aloud while using your hands to show the numbers. And you need to listen, so you can describe what Peter told a crowd they needed to do to follow Jesus.**

(Have your Bible open to Acts 2. Display the story figures as indicated.) We know that Jesus died on a cross, but came back to life. For **40** *(kids count by tens)* days, Jesus *(1a)* was with His followers *(7a).* Jesus proved that He was alive, and He spoke to them about the kingdom of God.

But the day came for Jesus to leave earth to return to Heaven. As His followers watched, Jesus was lifted off the ground. *(Remove 1a.)* **Two** *(kids count)* angels said to the followers that Jesus would someday come back in the same way He had left.

The followers of Jesus stayed together. They prayed and waited for the Holy Spirit whom Jesus had promised. **Ten** *(kids count)* days after Jesus went to Heaven, a huge crowd gathered in Jerusalem *(Show 5b, 6b.)* People came from many different countries to celebrate a special time called Pentecost. But the followers of Jesus didn't join in the celebration. They waited together for the Holy Spirit.

The Holy Spirit did come! The house where the followers were was filled with a noise like a violent wind. Something like flames of fire stood over each follower. The Holy Spirit had come upon Jesus' followers. They could now speak about Jesus in different languages. The people were amazed to hear Jesus' followers speaking in their own languages.

(Show Teaching Picture 7.) Then Peter stood up with the other **11** *(kids count)* followers and began to speak in a loud voice. Peter preached the good news that Jesus is alive even though He had been killed. When Peter was done

Explore His Word (continued)

Life Focus
❤ We can follow Jesus.

preaching about Jesus, the people were desperate to know what to do. They asked, "What shall we do?"

Peter answered, "Repent and be baptized, every one of you, in the name of Jesus Christ for the forgiveness of your sins. And you will receive the gift of the Holy Spirit" (2:38).

About **3,000** *(count by thousands)* people did exactly what Peter said. Those people were happy to be part of Jesus' church. The day of Pentecost was a very special day for Jesus' church.

These new followers of Jesus continued to meet together. They learned more about Jesus. They ate together. They remembered Jesus with the Lord's Supper, and they prayed together.

Bible Review Activity

On what special day did Peter tell a large crowd about following Jesus? (Pentecost) **Let's see what else you remember from the story.** Have the children sit in a circle and pass Peter's headpiece until you say "Peter preached!" The child holding the headpiece can put it on and answer a review question. Be sure that each child has the opportunity to answer a question. For more questions about the story, see the Review Questions on the CD.

• **For whom did Jesus' followers wait and pray after Jesus went back into Heaven?** (Holy Spirit)
• **What did the Holy Spirit help the followers do?** (speak in different languages)
• **What follower of Jesus preached the good news about Jesus?** (Peter)
• **What did the people ask after Peter was done preaching about Jesus?** ("What shall we do?")
• **What did Peter tell the people they needed to do?** (repent and be baptized)
• **How many people repented and were baptized?** (about 3,000)
• **What did the followers of Jesus continue to do?** (met together, learned about Jesus, ate together, took the Lord's Supper, prayed together)

The church, those people who believed in Jesus, followed Jesus. We're learning that ❤ we can follow Jesus too.

Bible Skill Builder and Bible Memory Activity

Write "Acts 4:19, 20" on the board. **Turn in your Bibles to the table of contents.** Give children time to do so. **Look in the New Testament section. Matthew is the first book of the New Testament. What's the next book?** (Mark) **The next book?** (Luke) **The next book?** (John) **These first four books of the New Testament tell about Jesus. What's the next book?** (Acts) **Acts tells about the early years of Jesus' church.** Help the children find Acts 4:19, 20 in their Bibles. Ask for volunteers to read the verses.

Before class, make copies of the words for "Judge for Yourselves." Distribute copies of the words and play "Judge for Yourselves." (Note: The recorded Bible Memory activity is based on the *New International Version* © 1984.) Go over the suggested motions with the children. Play the rhythm again and invite kids to join in.

Our Bible Memory tells how Peter and John chose to obey God even when it was hard. They also chose to tell others about Jesus. That's what a follower of Jesus does. Let's decide today that ❤ we can follow Jesus too!

Materials
Resources Sheet 6
Peter's headpiece,
CD Review Questions
printable file

Materials
white board, dry-erase marker, Bibles, *Resources* CD Track 11 and "Judge for Yourselves" Posters and Activities printable file, CD player

Teaching Tip
Print and use the Unit 2 Bible Skills Worksheets found on the *Resources* CD to help children name the first five books of the New Testament.

Life Focus
❤ We can follow Jesus.

Make It Real (15 minutes)

Step 3 • Use one of these activities to help children **identify times to follow Jesus.**

Materials
Activities p. 22, colored pencils or markers

Activity Page

Expert Tip
You shouldn't ask a child to do anything you wouldn't do. . . . Want kids to change and live differently? How has the lesson changed you?
—*Rick Chromey*

Materials
Resources Sheet 5 picture cards for Lesson 7

Act It Out

Materials
Weekly Bible Reader® Issue 7

LISTEN

Quick Step Following Jesus
The early followers of Jesus became the church. They learned what it meant to follow Jesus. Let's identify times ❤ we can follow Jesus. Distribute the activity pages and colored pencils or markers. Read the directions aloud and do the page together. Ask for a volunteer to read the first situation. Ask for another volunteer to tell which picture shows what Evan should do since he wants to follow Jesus. (forgiving Alex) Do the same with the other two rows.
• **When are some other times ❤ we can follow Jesus?** (when we show love for others, when we read the Bible, when we help others, when we tell the truth, when we do our best, when we share, when we pray, when we learn about Jesus, when we obey parents and teachers)
There are lots of times ❤ we can follow Jesus. In fact, ❤ we can follow Jesus all the time!

Option Times to Follow
The early followers of Jesus became the church. They learned what it meant to follow Jesus. Let's identify times ❤ we can follow Jesus. Give each of the picture cards to an individual child, a pair of children, or a small group of children. **Look at the picture you have and read the question. Decide together how you can follow Jesus and then decide how to act it out.** As needed, help the children with reading the text on their cards and with ideas how to act out their situations. As each child or group acts out his situation, the rest of the class can decide what he is doing.
• **When are some other times ❤ we can follow Jesus?** (when we read the Bible, when we do our best, when we share, when we pray, when we learn about Jesus)
As we go throughout each day, let's think of times ❤ we can follow Jesus.

Option Story from *Weekly Bible Reader®*
The early followers of Jesus became the church. They learned what it meant to follow Jesus. Let's identify times ❤ we can follow Jesus. Read "I Guess I Did!"
• **When are some times ❤ we can follow Jesus?** (See the activities above for possible responses.)
There are lots of times ❤ we can follow Jesus. In fact, ❤ we can follow Jesus all the time!

Live It Out (10 minutes)

Life Focus
❤ We can follow Jesus.

Step 4 • Use one of these activities to help children **choose a time they will follow Jesus.**

≡ Quick Step   What We Can Do

We've learned that there are lots of times each day that ❤ we can follow Jesus. Now it's time for you to choose at least one time that you will follow Jesus. Attach the title card, "Here Is What We Can Do!" to a bulletin board or wall. Attach the Lesson 7 card under the title. Read the text aloud on both cards.

Distribute construction paper and crayons. Ask kids to trace one of their feet on paper and then cut them out. Have kids write or draw pictures of at least one time they will follow Jesus. When kids are done, let them share the times they plan to follow Jesus. Then they can attach their "following feet" under the Lesson 7 card.

Have kids gather for a time of prayer. Invite children to pray for God's help to follow Jesus each day.

Option   Time to Follow Game

We've learned that there are lots of times each day that ❤ we can follow Jesus. Now it's time for you to choose a time that you will follow Jesus. Have the children sit in a circle. **As a reminder that Peter told the people about Jesus and about 3,000 people became part of Jesus' church, we're going to pass this picture around the circle. Keep passing the picture until I say "Time to follow!" If I say "Time to follow!" and you are holding the picture, name a time you will follow Jesus.** Be sure that everyone gets a turn to tell a time they plan on following Jesus.

Close with a prayer circle. Ask each child to name the time he mentioned in the game that he will follow Jesus. Then lead the class in prayer. **Dear God, please help ___ (name of child) follow Jesus ___ (time child named). In Jesus' name, amen.** Ask all children to name times they will follow Jesus and then pray for each of the children in the same manner. After the prayer, remind children: **As you go throughout each day, remember that ❤ we can follow Jesus.**

Saying Good-bye

• Distribute Issue 7 of *Weekly Bible Reader*® and the *Activities* page 31 Unit 2 Bible Memory poster and stickers. Stickers are in the middle of *Early Elementary Activities*. Encourage kids to complete their posters at home by adding the stickers and coloring.

• Make sure children have projects and activity sheets they have done.

• If you have time before parents arrive, use some of the activities on page 58.

• Be sure parents know about the *Faith & Family* page available online to download and use at home. You may want to print and have a copy on display for parents to see. Go to www.heartshaper.com.

Materials
Resources Sheet 8 "Here Is What We Can Do!" title card and card for Lesson 7, pushpins or reusable adhesive, construction paper, crayons, markers, scissors

Art

Materials
Teaching Picture 7

Game

Evaluate
• How eager were the children to follow Jesus?
• How did you give attention to the children who are very quiet?

Peter and John at the Temple

8

Bible Focus: Acts 3:1-19

Bible Memory: But Peter and John replied, "Which is right in God's eyes: to listen to you, or to him? You be the judges! As for us, we cannot help speaking about what we have seen and heard" (Acts 4:19, 20).

Life Focus: ❤ We can tell others about Jesus.

Heart to Heart

Peter seems to be a single-minded man. After healing the man at the temple, he, along with John, took the opportunity to tell about Jesus. When put in prison because of this, Peter ends up telling the jailer about Jesus. When later put in chains and guarded by soldiers in Rome, Peter tells about Jesus.

Sometimes we are single-minded. But some of us may be single-minded about making more money. Or some may be single-minded about having a beautiful home. Or some may be single-minded about a job and working long hours. Take some time and discover what you may be single-minded about. Hopefully, both you and God will be pleased.

Lesson 8 at a Glance

			HeartShaper Materials	Other Materials
Step 1 **Focus In** Use one of these activities to help children *explore telling messages.*	☰ *Quick Step* The Telephone Game **Option** Signing Messages	Game / Sign Language	• none • none	• none • none
	Bible Memory *Use this activity to introduce the Bible Memory verses.*	DISCUSS	• *Resources* CD including the "Judge for Yourselves" printable file (*NIV* or *KJV*)	• Bible, CD player
Step 2 **Explore His Word** Use all of these activities to help children *describe times Peter and John told about Jesus* and develop Bible skills.	Peter and John at the Temple **Bible Review Activity** **Bible Skill Builder and Bible Memory Activity**	Bible Story / Music / Bible Skills	• *Resources* Sheet 6 Peter and John headpieces and Bible Memory poster, Sheet 8 name card and card 8a, CD; *Teaching Picture* 8; *Activities* p. 23	• white board, dry-erase marker, Bibles, yarn, hole punch, clear tape, pencils, CD player, reusable adhesive
Step 3 **Make It Real** Use one of these activities to help children *discover ways to tell about Jesus.*	☰ *Quick Step* Ways to Tell About Jesus Option Go Tell Game **Option** Story from *Weekly Bible Reader®*	Activity Page / Game / LISTEN	• *Activities* p. 24 and corresponding stickers • *Resources* Sheet 7 game board • *Weekly Bible Reader®* Issue 8	• none • small items to use as game markers, coin • none
Step 4 **Live It Out** Use one of these activities to help children *plan a way they will tell about Jesus.*	☰ *Quick Step* Book About Jesus **Option** What We Can Do Saying Good-bye	Craft / Art	• reproducible p. 95 • *Resources* Sheet 8 title card and cards for Lessons 7 and 8 • *Weekly Bible Reader®* Issue 8	• markers or colored pencils, scissors, construction paper, glue • pushpins or reusable adhesive, paper, markers • none

Focus In (15 minutes)

Step 1 • Use one of these activities to help children **explore telling messages.** Use the Bible Memory activity to introduce the memory verses.

Welcome
- Welcome each child by name.
- Do check-in procedures you follow (name and security tags, offering, attendance chart, etc.).
- Early arrivers will enjoy doing one or more of the activities described on page 58.

≡ *Quick Step* The Telephone Game

Today we're going to explore telling messages. Have kids gather in a circle for the game. Tell kids they are going to play the Telephone game. Whisper this message in the ear of one child: ❤ **We can tell others about Jesus.** That child should whisper that message to the next child. Then each child whispers whatever she hears to the next child. Ask the last child to say aloud what she heard. Tell kids if that's the message you said to the first child. Try other messages, such as: Jesus is the Son of God and died on the cross for us. God loved the world so much that He sent Jesus.

• **What are some ways to tell messages?** (talk, letters and cards, e-mail, telephone, draw a picture, sign language)

These are all ways to tell messages. Most of these are ways that ❤ we can tell others about Jesus.

Materials
none

Game

Option Signing Messages

Today we're going to explore telling messages. How can we tell messages to people who can't hear? (use sign language) **Let's learn to say ❤ "We can tell others about Jesus" in sign language.** Lead kids in doing these signs: *we*—move the index finger from one shoulder to the other; *tell*—the index finger starts under the chin and is thrust outward; *others*—make a fist with the thumb up and point to someone with the thumb; *Jesus*—touch the middle finger of one hand to the middle of the palm of the other hand and then repeat with the other hand.

Now let's say "We can follow Jesus" in sign language. Lead kids in doing these signs: *we*—(see above); *follow*—with both thumbs up and hands in fists, put the right hand against the left hand, but slightly behind it, and push outward; *Jesus*—(see above).

• **What are some other ways to tell messages?** (talk, letters and cards, e-mail, telephone, draw a picture)

These are all ways to tell messages. Most of these are ways that ❤ we can tell others about Jesus.

Materials
none

Sign Language

Bible Memory Acts 4:19, 20

Read aloud Acts 4:19, 20 from the Bible. **Who did Peter and John know that it was always right to listen to?** (God) **Peter and John knew they would be obeying God when they told others about Jesus. And they *always* told others about Jesus. They couldn't help it! Whom can you tell about Jesus?** (Let kids respond.) Play "Judge for Yourselves" and invite kids to join in. Words and motions can be found in a printable file on the CD. **We can be like Peter and John when we tell others about Jesus.**

Materials
Bible, *Resources* CD Track 11 and the "Judge for Yourselves" Posters and Activities printable file (*NIV* or *KJV*), CD player

DISCUSS

Transition to Explore His Word
See the *Resources* CD Transition Tips printable file. As children gather, make sure you have all the materials you need.

Life Focus
♥ We can tell others about Jesus.

Step 2 • Use all of these activities to help children **describe times Peter and John told about Jesus** and develop Bible skills.

Bible Background for the Teacher

The temple gate called Beautiful was likely what historian Josephus described as being made with brass and 75 feet high. This gate was a favorite entrance to the temple court.

At the time of this event, people with disabilities did not have any opportunities to earn money and there were no assistance programs. Many times these people begged for money in order to buy food.

When Peter said, "In the name of Jesus Christ of Nazareth," he was not using Jesus' name as though it was some kind of magic word. Rather, Peter was letting everyone know that this power to heal was coming from God. Jesus' disciples did many miracles so that people would know their message was from God (see John 10:37, 38; 1 Corinthians 2:3-5). When the man who could not walk could suddenly leap and jump, it was further proof that God had caused this miraculous healing; it was not a natural healing.

Peter's remarks to the crowd may sound harsh—"You killed Jesus"—but his overall message was actually one of hope. Peter was letting the people of Israel know that God wanted to forgive them if they would now believe that Jesus was God's Son who had died for them.

Worship Time
If you want to offer a time of worship, see the *Resources* CD Worship Time Ideas printable file for suggestions.

Materials
white board; dry-erase marker; Bibles; *Resources* Sheet 6 Peter and John headpieces, Sheet 8 "man who could not walk" name card and card 8a; yarn; hole punch; clear tape; *Teaching Picture* 8

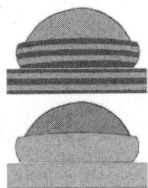

Bible Story

man who could not walk

Before Class
Put together John's headpiece as described on Sheet 6. Punch two holes in the "man who could not walk" name card and string with yarn.

Peter and John at the Temple (Acts 3:1-19)

Write "Matthew, Mark, Luke, John" on the board. **The New Testament part of the Bible starts with these four books.** Point to the names as you say them. Ask the children to say them with you. Write "Acts 3:1" on the board. **Our Bible story comes from the book of Acts. Do you think Acts comes before Matthew or after John?** (after John) Help children turn to Acts 3:1 in their Bibles and ask for a volunteer to read the verse.

Choose two children to wear the Peter and John headpieces and act out what these men did. Choose a child to wear the "man who could not walk" name card and act out what that man did. **You all need to be involved in today's Bible story. Each time you hear about Peter and John telling about Jesus, raise your hand and then put it back down.**

(Have your Bible open to Acts 3.) One day soon after Pentecost, Peter and John went to the temple to pray. It was 3:00 in the afternoon. This was the time every day that they had a prayer service at the temple.

One of the gates of the temple was called Beautiful. By that gate was a man who could not walk. Every day some people carried the man to the gate so he could beg for money. When the man saw Peter and John, he begged them to give him some money *(show card 8a)*.

Peter and John looked at the man. Then Peter said something the man did not expect to hear. "Look at us," Peter said. "Silver or gold I do not have, but what I do have I give you. In the name of **Jesus** Christ of Nazareth, walk" (v. 6; *kids should raise hands*).

Then Peter took the man's hand and helped him stand up. *(Show Teaching Picture 8.)* Immediately the man's feet and ankles felt different—they became strong. He jumped up and began to walk. Can you imagine how excited he must have been?

The man followed Peter and John into the temple. The man was not only walking, but he was also jumping and praising God. He was so excited that a crowd began to form.

The people knew the man. He was the one who begged for money at the

Explore His Word (continued)

gate called Beautiful. Now he was walking and praising God. Everyone was amazed! How could this have happened?

The crowd gathered around Peter and John. Peter began to tell them about **Jesus**. *(Kids should raise hands.)* Peter said, "You killed Jesus but God raised Him from the dead. By faith in the name of **Jesus**, this man has been made strong. *(Kids should raise hands.)* He is completely healed. You need to repent and come back to God." That day many people heard about Jesus.

Bible Review Activity

When are some times Peter and John told about Jesus? (When they healed the man who couldn't walk. When they told the crowd that the power of Jesus had healed the man.) **Let's see what else you remember from the story.** Distribute the activity pages and pencils. Read the directions aloud and do the page together.

Let's sing a fun song that tells about Peter and John and the man who couldn't walk. Play "Silver and Gold Have I None." Explain a few words in the song: *lame* means "unable to walk" and *alms* means "money." Play the song again and invite children to join in singing. The song is also a fun one to act out while singing.

Peter and John told everyone about Jesus. ❤ **We can tell others about Jesus too!**

Materials
Activities p. 23, pencils, *Resources* CD Tracks 7 and 8, CD player

Music

Bible Skill Builder and Bible Memory Activity

Write "Matthew, Mark, Luke, John, Acts" on the board. **Are Matthew, Mark, Luke, John, and Acts the first five books of the Old Testament or the New Testament?** (New) Point to the names as you lead kids in saying the names a couple times. Erase "Mark." Point to the names and the blank space as you lead kids in saying the names again. Erase "John" and do the same. Write "Acts 4:19, 20" on the board. Help the children find Acts 4:19, 20 in their Bibles and ask for volunteers to read the verses.

Display the Bible Memory poster. Point to the words as you read them aloud. Do the same again but invite kids to join you in reading the Bible Memory verses. Press apart the sections of the poster and shuffle them. Ask kids to put the poster back in the right order. Ask everyone to join in reading the Bible Memory verses together.

Peter and John were always telling people about Jesus. ❤ **We can tell others about Jesus too!**

Materials
white board, dry-erase marker, Bibles, *Resources* Sheet 6 Bible Memory poster, reusable adhesive

Bible Skills

Life Focus
❤ We can tell others about Jesus.

Make It Real (15 minutes)

Step 3 • Use one of these activities to help children **discover ways to tell about Jesus.**

Materials
Activities p. 24 and corresponding stickers

Activity Page

≡ *Quick Step* Ways to Tell About Jesus
We want to be like Peter and John and tell about Jesus. Let's discover ways ❤ we can tell others about Jesus. Distribute the activity pages and stickers. Read the directions aloud and do the page together.
Ask for a volunteer to read the first sentence. **Look at your stickers.**
• **What sticker should we put in the empty space?** (mouth)
Ask for a volunteer to read the second sentence.
• **What sticker should we put in the empty space?** (book) Do the same for all the sentences.
• **What are some ways ❤ we can tell others about Jesus?** (use the phone or send an e-mail and invite a friend to come to Sunday school to learn about Jesus, pray before meals and tell friends why you do that, make something that tells about Jesus and share it with a friend, talk to a friend and tell her about Jesus)
There are lots of ways ❤ we can tell others about Jesus. I hope we can all use lots of these ways to tell others about Jesus.

Materials
Resources Sheet 7 game board, small items to use as game markers, coin

Game

Option Go Tell Game
We want to be like Peter and John and tell about Jesus. Let's discover ways ❤ we can tell others about Jesus as we play a fun game. Put out the game board and allow children to choose game markers. Children can toss a coin to move spaces on the board: heads, they can move one space; tails, they can move two spaces. Help children as needed to read the text as they land on spaces and help them with responses. When the game is over, ask:
• **What are some ways ❤ we can tell others about Jesus?** (use the phone or send an e-mail and invite a friend to come to Sunday school to learn about Jesus, pray before meals and tell friends why you do that, make something that tells about Jesus and share it with a friend, talk to a friend and tell her about Jesus)
There are lots of ways ❤ we can tell others about Jesus.

Materials
Weekly Bible Reader® Issue 8

LISTEN

Option Story from *Weekly Bible Reader®*
We want to be like Peter and John and tell about Jesus. Let's discover ways ❤ we can tell others about Jesus. Read "Alisha and Zoe."
• **When are some times ❤ we can tell others about Jesus?** (See the activities above for possible responses.)
There are lots of ways ❤ we can tell others about Jesus. I hope we can all use lots of these ways to tell others about Jesus.

Live It Out (10 minutes)

Step 4 • Use one of these activities to help children **plan a way they will tell about Jesus.**

☰ *Quick Step* Book About Jesus

We've discovered lots of ways to tell about Jesus. One way ❤ we can tell others about Jesus is to make something that tells about Jesus and share it with them. Let's make books about Jesus that you can share with someone.

Before class, make copies of the reproducible page. Distribute the pages and supplies. Kids can first color and then cut out the pictures and word boxes. Show children how to fold a sheet of construction paper into fourths to make a book. Kids can glue the word box *Jesus is the Son of God* on the cover and then glue the other pictures and word box wherever they desire.

Ask children to bring their completed books to a closing prayer circle. Demonstrate handing one of the books to someone. Say, **Here's a book I made about Jesus.** Point to the pictures as you say, **Jesus loves children. Jesus fed a huge crowd with just a little lunch.** Put children in pairs or small groups. Using their books, guide kids to practice telling each other about Jesus. Close with prayer, asking for God's help to tell others about Jesus.

Materials
reproducible p. 95, markers or colored pencils, scissors, construction paper, glue

Craft

Option   What We Can Do

We've discovered lots of ways to tell about Jesus. Now you are going to plan a way you will tell about Jesus. If you did not attach the title card, "Here Is What We Can Do!" and Lesson 7 card on a bulletin board or wall in Lesson 7, you can do so now. Then attach the Lesson 8 card on the board or wall. Read the text aloud on all the cards. Distribute paper and markers. Ask kids to draw at least one way they plan on telling others about Jesus. Remind kids of the ways to tell about Jesus they discovered in Step 3. When kids are finished, have them share what they drew. Encourage them to follow through on their plans. Then they can attach their papers under the Lesson 8 card.

Have children gather for a time of prayer. Encourage children to pray and ask for God's help in telling others about Jesus.

Materials
Resources Sheet 8 "Here Is What We Can Do!" title card and cards for Lessons 7 and 8, pushpins or reusable adhesive, paper, markers

Art

Saying Good-bye

• Distribute Issue 8 of *Weekly Bible Reader*®.
• Make sure children have projects and activity sheets they have done.
• If you have time before parents arrive, use some of the activities on page 58.
• Remind parents that a weekly *Faith & Family* page is available online to print and use with their child at home. See www.heartshaper.com.

Evaluate
• How eager were the children to tell about Jesus?
• How joyful and eager are you in telling the children about Jesus?

Peter and John Speak Boldly

Bible Focus: Acts 4:1-31

Bible Memory: But Peter and John replied, "Which is right in God's eyes: to listen to you, or to him? You be the judges! As for us, we cannot help speaking about what we have seen and heard" (Acts 4:19, 20).

Life Focus: ❤ We can speak boldly about Jesus.

Heart to Heart

The Bible tells us that Peter and John could not keep quiet—they had to talk about Jesus. Can't you just picture these two men telling everyone they met about Jesus? If they went to an outdoor market, they told the vendors about Jesus. If they saw a man who couldn't walk, they healed him and talked to him about Jesus. If they went on a journey to another town, they told everyone they met about Jesus.

These ordinary men's lives had been transformed, and they were no longer satisfied to talk about ordinary things. How about you? Pray for boldness to talk about Jesus with the children in your class, your friends, your family, and with anyone you meet.

Lesson 9 at a Glance

			HeartShaper Materials	Other Materials
Step 1 **Focus In** Use one of these activities to help children *explore what* boldly *means.*	*Quick Step* Boldly Jump Up!	*Action*	• none	• none
	Option Being Bold	*Act It Out*	• none	• paper, pencil
	Bible Memory *Use this activity to introduce the Bible Memory verses.*	*Discuss*	• none	• Bible
Step 2 **Explore His Word** Use all of these activities to help children *tell what Peter and John and the believers asked of God* and develop Bible skills.	Peter and John Speak Boldly	*Bible Story*	• *Resources* Sheet 6 Peter and John headpieces, Sheet 8 name card and cards 9a and 9b, CD Review Questions and "Judge for Yourselves" printable files; *Teaching Picture* 9	• white board, dry-erase marker, Bibles, hole punch, yarn, paper, marker, CD player
	Bible Review Activity	*Action*		
	Bible Skill Builder and Bible Memory Activity	*Bible Skills*		
Step 3 **Make It Real** Use one of these activities to help children *identify times to speak boldly about Jesus.*	*Quick Step* Puppet Fun	*Activity Page*	• *Activities* p. 25	• markers, scissors, paper lunch bags, glue
	Option Go Tell Game	*Game*	• *Resources* Sheet 7 game board	• small items to use as game markers, coin
	Option Story from *Weekly Bible Reader®*	*Listen*	• *Weekly Bible Reader®* Issue 9	• none
Step 4 **Live It Out** Use one of these activities to help children *ask for God's help so they can speak boldly about Jesus.*	*Quick Step* Prayers for Boldness	*Pray*	• none	• none
	Option What We Can Do	*Art*	• *Resources* Sheet 8 title card and cards for Lessons 7–9	• pushpins or reusable adhesive, construction paper, markers or crayons, scissors
	Saying Good-bye		• *Weekly Bible Reader®* Issue 9	• none

Focus In (15 minutes)

Step 1 • Use one of these activities to help children **explore what** *boldly* **means.** Use the Bible Memory activity to introduce the memory verses.

Welcome
- Welcome each child by name.
- Do check-in procedures you follow (name and security tags, offering, attendance chart, etc.).
- Early arrivers will enjoy doing one or more of the activities described on page 58.

Quick Step Boldly Jump Up!

Let's think about what the word *boldly* **means.** Tell the children that you will read several sentences. If a sentence describes someone acting boldly, they are to jump up and say boldly "That's bold!" If a sentence does not describe someone acting boldly, they should not jump up or say anything.

The firefighter ran into the burning house to save the children. (That's bold!)

Several girls were teasing Sarah's friend. Sarah ran and didn't help her friend. (not bold)

The police officer helped the people to safety even though he was in danger himself. (That's bold!)

Dylan wanted to tell his friend about Jesus, but he knew his friend might laugh at him. Dylan told him anyway. (That's bold!)

Emma wanted to speak up during class about something she really believed in. But she didn't do it. (not bold)

- **What does the word** *boldly* **mean?** (to not be afraid to do something)

We're going to learn today that ❤ we can speak boldly about Jesus.

Materials

Added Fun!

Let kids make up situations to tell the rest of the class.

Option Being Bold

What do you think the word *boldly* **means?** (Accept children's responses.) Before class, write the following on separate slips of paper: A firefighter runs into a burning house to save children. Your friend is being teased and you don't help him. A police officer protects people from someone who is trying to hurt them. You keep telling a friend about Jesus even though the friend laughs at you. You want to speak up during class about something you believe in, but you don't do it.

Ask for a volunteer to choose a slip of paper and act out the situation. He can choose a friend or two to help him act it out. The rest of the class can guess what is happening. Be sure that everyone gets the opportunity to participate. After the class guesses what each situation is, ask:

- **Was the person bold? Why or why not?**
- **What does the word** *boldly* **mean?** (to not be afraid to do something)

We're going to learn today that ❤ we can speak boldly about Jesus.

Materials

paper, pencil

Bible Memory Acts 4:19, 20

Think about some things that you like to talk or speak about. When I say go, I want all of you to speak aloud about those things for the next minute. Go! Let the kids speak aloud for one minute. **Most of us like to talk. We talk about having fun, things we're doing, places we're going, and lots of other things.** Read aloud Acts 4:19, 20. **What did Peter and John like to speak about?** (things they had seen and heard while they traveled with Jesus, such as His miracles) **Peter and John knew what was important to speak about. I hope that we will learn that ❤ we can speak boldly about Jesus.**

Materials

Bible

Transition to Explore His Word

See the *Resources* CD Transition Tips printable file. As children gather, make sure you have all the materials you need.

Life Focus
❤ We can speak boldly about Jesus.

Explore His Word (20 minutes)

Step 2 • Use all of these activities to help children **tell what Peter and John and the believers asked of God** and develop Bible skills.

Bible Background for the Teacher

Here we see the disciples defying the Jewish leaders. The Jewish leaders did not want the men teaching about Jesus. The disciples knew that they should respect human authority. Yet when human authority and God's commands were not the same, the disciples choose God's way—even if it meant they would be punished.

Since the people had just witnessed the miracle performed on the man who could not walk, a warning to not preach about Jesus was all that the Jewish leaders felt they could do to Peter and John.

It's interesting that the believers did not pray to be delivered from their troubles or pray for God to harm the Jewish leaders who had thrown Peter and John into jail. Those who prayed for boldness were believers, which means they had already received the Holy Spirit (Ephesians 1:13; Titus 3:5). So what is this "filling of the Holy Spirit" that they received? There are other instances of believers being "filled with" the Holy Spirit in Scripture (Luke 1:15; Acts 2:4; 7:55; 13:9; 19:6). In this case, the believers prayed for boldness, and God gave them extra help to stand against opposition and speak boldly about Jesus.

Worship Time
If you want to offer a time of worship, see the *Resources* CD Worship Time Ideas printable file for suggestions.

Materials
white board; dry-erase marker; Bibles; *Resources* Sheet 6 Peter and John headpieces, Sheet 8 "Jewish leaders" name card and cards 9a and 9b; *Teaching Picture* 9; hole punch; yarn

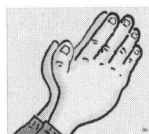

Before Class
Punch two holes in the "Jewish leaders" name card and string with yarn.

Peter and John Speak Boldly (Acts 4:1-31)

Write "Matthew, Mark, Luke, John" on the board. **The New Testament part of the Bible starts with these four books.** Point to the names as you read them aloud. Ask the children to say them with you. **These four books are called the Gospels, and they tell about Jesus. Our Bible story comes from the New Testament book of Acts.** Write "Acts 4:1" on the board after "John." Help children find Acts in the table of contents and then help them turn to Acts 4:1 in their Bibles. Ask for a volunteer to read the verse.

Choose two children to wear the Peter and John headpieces and act out what these men did. Choose a child to wear the "Jewish leaders" name card and act out what they did. **You all need to be involved in today's Bible story. When you hear the words** *speak, spoke,* **or** *speaking,* **do this sign: with an open hand, tap your mouth twice with your index finger. And everyone needs to listen for what Peter, John, and the believers asked of God.**

(Have your Bible open to Acts 4.) After Peter and John healed the man by the temple gate, they **spoke** *(kids do sign language)* to the crowd of people about Jesus. The Jewish leaders were upset because Peter and John were teaching the people about Jesus. The Jewish leaders and the captain of the temple guard grabbed Peter and John and threw them into jail *(show card 9a).* Since it was already night, the Jewish leaders kept them in jail until the next day.

So the next day, Peter and John were brought before the Jewish leaders. *(Show Teaching Picture 9.)*

The Jewish leaders asked, "Who gave you the power to heal this man?"

With the help of the Holy Spirit, Peter **spoke** to them about Jesus. Peter boldly told them that Jesus is God's Son and that God raised Jesus from the dead after He had been crucified. Peter also told them that the man at the temple gate was made well by faith in the name of Jesus.

The Jewish leaders told Peter and John, "You must not **speak** or teach about Jesus anymore."

But Peter and John answered them, "Which is right in God's eyes: to listen to you or to him? We cannot help **speaking** about what we have seen and heard."

The Jewish leaders did not know how to punish Peter and John. All the people were praising God for the miracle that had happened to the man by the temple gate. So the Jewish leaders warned Peter and John not to **speak** about Jesus anymore. Then Peter and John were let go.

Peter and John went to find their friends who believed in Jesus. Peter and John told their friends everything that had happened to them. All of the believers prayed together a very special prayer to God *(show card 9b)*. They prayed, "Lord, help us to **speak** Your word with great boldness. Help us to be brave by showing us Your power." They asked God to help them not to be afraid. They asked God to help them be bold so they could keep telling others about Jesus no matter what happened to them!

After the believers prayed, they were all filled with the Holy Spirit. They **spoke** God's word without fear. They boldly told everyone about Jesus.

Bible Review Activity

What did Peter, John, and the believers ask of God? (They asked God to help them be bold so they could keep telling others about Jesus no matter what happened to them!) Have the children sit in a circle and pass the Peter or John headpiece until you say "Be bold!" The child holding the headpiece can wear it while answering a review question. For more questions about the story, see the Review Questions on the CD.

• **What did the Jewish leaders do to Peter and John for speaking about Jesus?** (threw them into jail)

• **Whom did Peter tell the Jewish leaders about?** (Jesus)

• **What did the Jewish leaders tell Peter and John not to do?** (speak about Jesus)

• **For what did the believers pray?** (for boldness to speak about Jesus)

• **What happened after Peter, John, and the believers prayed?** (They were filled with the Holy Spirit and were not afraid to speak about Jesus.)

Peter, John, and the believers asked for God's help to spoke boldly about Jesus. We need to ask for God's help too, so ❤ we can speak boldly about Jesus.

Bible Skill Builder and Bible Memory Activity

Before class, print the names of the first five books of the New Testament on separate sheets of paper. **I need four volunteers to hold these signs in order** (Matthew, Mark, Luke, John). **These are the names of the first four books of the New Testament—Matthew, Mark, Luke, and John.** Lead the children in saying the names together. Ask the kids to close their eyes while you rearrange the kids with the name signs. **Time to open your eyes. What's wrong?** Ask for a volunteer to put the books in order again. Repeat as time allows. Write "Acts 4:19, 20" on the board. Have a child hold up the Acts name sign. **Where should we put the book of Acts?** (after John) Help the children turn to Acts 4:19, 20 in their Bibles and ask for volunteers to read the verses.

Before class, make copies of the words for "Judge for Yourselves." Distribute copies of the words. Go over the suggested motions, play "Judge for Yourselves," and invite kids to join in. **Peter and John weren't afraid to speak boldly about Jesus. Remember that ❤ we can speak boldly about Jesus too.**

Materials

Action

Resources Sheet 6
Peter's or John's headpiece, CD Review Questions printable file

Materials

Bible Skills

paper, marker, white board, dry-erase marker, Bibles, *Resources* CD Track 11 and "Judge for Yourselves" Posters and Activities printable file, CD player

Teaching Tip

Print and use the Unit 2 Bible Skills Worksheets found on the *Resources* CD to help children name the first five books of the New Testament.

Life Focus

❤ We can speak boldly about Jesus.

Make It Real (15 minutes)

Step 3 • Use one of these activities to help children **identify times to speak boldly about Jesus.**

Materials

Activities p. 25, markers, scissors, paper lunch bags, glue

Activity Page

Added Fun!

Provide yarn for kids to use as hair for their puppets.

≡ *Quick Step* Puppet Fun

We want to be like Peter and John and speak boldly about Jesus. Distribute the activity pages and supplies. Read the directions aloud. Help the children as needed to make their paper bag puppets.

Ask the kids to hold their puppets. **Help your puppets speak boldly about Jesus by saying "Jesus died for us and then rose from the dead."** Laugh a little and ask, **What do you mean that Jesus rose from the dead? That's not possible.** Lead the children to use their puppets in saying "It is possible. Jesus is God's Son." **Jesus, God's Son?** Laugh a little. **I don't think I want to talk to you anymore. I don't like to hear about this Jesus.** Lead the children to use their puppets in saying "I love you and Jesus does too." As time permits, let kids put on puppet shows, having their puppets speak boldly about Jesus.

• **When are some times that ❤ we can speak boldly about Jesus?** (when we're with friends who don't know about Jesus, when people make fun of us for speaking about Jesus, when someone may not like us for telling about Jesus)

Let's be like Peter and John. Let's remember that ❤ we can speak boldly about Jesus.

Materials

Resources Sheet 7 game board, small items to use as game markers, coin

Game

Option   Go Tell Game

We want to be like Peter and John and speak boldly about Jesus. Let's discover ways ❤ we can speak boldly about Jesus as we play a fun game. Lay out the game board and allow children to choose game markers. Children can toss a coin to move spaces on the board: heads, they can move one space; tails, they can move two spaces. Help children as needed to read the text as they land on spaces and help them with responses. When the game is over, ask:

• **When are some times that ❤ we can speak boldly about Jesus?** (when we're with friends who don't know about Jesus, when people make fun of us for speaking about Jesus, when someone may not like us for telling about Jesus)

We want to be like Peter and John. Remember that ❤ we can speak boldly about Jesus.

Materials

Weekly Bible Reader® Issue 9

LISTEN

Option   Story from *Weekly Bible Reader®*

We want to be like Peter and John and speak boldly about Jesus. Let's discover ways ❤ we can speak boldly about Jesus. Read "The Bus Ride."

• **When are some times ❤ we can speak boldly about Jesus?** (See the activities above for possible responses.)

Let's be like Peter and John. Let's remember that ❤ we can speak boldly about Jesus.

Live It Out (10 minutes)

❤ We can speak boldly about Jesus.

Step 4 • Use one of these activities to help children **ask for God's help so they can speak boldly about Jesus.**

▤ *Quick Step* Prayers for Boldness

We've identified times ❤ **we can speak boldly about Jesus. The only way we can speak boldly about Jesus is to pray for God's help. Let's pray and ask God to give us boldness to tell others about Jesus. We're going to use some of the same words that Peter, John, and the believers used when they prayed and asked God for boldness.**

Have children gather for a prayer time. Tell kids to repeat the prayer sentences after you have prayed them. **Dear God** (pause; kids repeat), **You made the heavens and the earth** (pause; kids repeat). **You made the seas and everything in them** (pause; kids repeat). **Help us to speak Your word with great boldness** (pause; kids repeat). **Help us to speak boldly about Jesus** (pause; kids repeat) **even when people make fun of us** (pause; kids repeat). **Help us to speak boldly about Jesus** (pause; kids repeat) **even when others may not like us** (pause; kids repeat). **Thank You for helping us speak boldly for You** (pause; kids repeat). **In Jesus' name, amen.**

Materials
none

Option What We Can Do

We've identified times ❤ **we can speak boldly about Jesus.** If you did not attach the title card "Here Is What We Can Do!" and Lessons 7 and 8 cards on a bulletin board or wall in Lessons 7 and/or 8, you can do so now. Then attach the Lesson 9 card on the board or wall. Read the text aloud on all the cards.

Distribute the construction paper and markers or crayons. Have each kid trace one of his hands and then cut it out. **These hands can remind us that we need to pray and ask for God's help in speaking boldly about Him. If you want to be like Peter and John and speak boldly about Jesus, sign your name on your hand outline.** Have kids attach their hand outlines by the Lesson 9 card. **The only way we can speak boldly about Jesus is to pray for God's help.**

Have kids gather for a time of prayer. Encourage kids to pray and ask for God's help in speaking boldly about Jesus. You may want to suggest that the children pray something similar to this: "Dear God, please help me to speak boldly about Jesus. In Jesus' name, amen."

Materials
Resources Sheet 8 "Here Is What We Can Do!" title card and cards for Lessons 7–9, pushpins or reusable adhesive, construction paper, markers or crayons, scissors

Saying Good-bye

• Distribute Issue 9 of *Weekly Bible Reader*®.
• Make sure children have projects and activity sheets they have done.
• If you have time before parents arrive, use some of the activities on page 58.
• Remind parents that a weekly *Faith & Family* page is available online to print and use with their child at home. See www.heartshaper.com.

Evaluate
• How willing are the children to speak to others about Jesus?
• How did you demonstrate care and concern for the children in your class?

Peter and John Speak Boldly, Lesson 9

Philip Teaches a Man from Ethiopia 10

Bible Focus: Acts 8:26-40
Bible Memory: But Peter and John replied, "Which is right in God's eyes: to listen to you, or to him? You be the judges! As for us, we cannot help speaking about what we have seen and heard" (Acts 4:19, 20).
Life Focus: ❤ We can know and understand God's Word.

Heart to Heart

Think about the people who have helped you know and understand God's Word. Did your mom or dad help you? Did Sunday school teachers help you? Did friends help you? Did a preacher help you? For many of us, the answer would probably be yes to many or all of the above.

Jesus' disciples, including Philip, seemed to take every possible opportunity to help people know and understand God's Word. Now it's your opportunity. You have already made yourself available to God, so He can work through you. Continue to study His Word. Keep learning. And keep shaping young hearts with God's Word. You too will rejoice!

Lesson 10 at a Glance

		HeartShaper Materials	Other Materials
Step 1 **Focus In** Use one of these activities to help children *explore things they know and understand.*	*Quick Step* What Do You Know?	• *Resources* Sheet 7 picture cards for Lesson 10	• none
	Option If You Know	• none	• none
	Bible Memory *Use this activity to introduce the Bible Memory verses.*	• *Resources* CD including the "Judge for Yourselves" printable file (*NIV* or *KJV*)	• Bible, CD player
Step 2 **Explore His Word** Use all of these activities to help children *tell how Philip helped the man from Ethiopia understand God's Word* and develop Bible skills.	Philip Teaches a Man from Ethiopia	• *Resources* Sheet 6 Bible Memory poster, Sheet 7 pictures 10a, 10b, CD Review Questions; *Teaching Picture* 10; *Activities* p. 27 and stickers	• white board, dry-erase marker, Bibles, coins, paper lunch bag, reusable adhesive
	Bible Review Activity		
	Bible Skill Builder and Bible Memory Activity		
Step 3 **Make It Real** Use one of these activities to help children *discover what or who can help them understand God's Word.*	*Quick Step* Who or What Can Help?	• *Activities* p. 28	• colored pencils or markers
	Option Drawing Game	• none	• paper, pencil, white board, dry-erase markers and eraser
	Option Story from *Weekly Bible Reader*	• *Weekly Bible Reader®* Issue 10	• none
Step 4 **Live It Out** Use one of these activities to help children *plan ways to better understand God's Word.*	*Quick Step* What We Can Do	• *Resources* Sheet 8 title card and cards for Lessons 7–10	• pushpins or reusable adhesive, construction paper, markers
	Option Scroll Reminders	• none	• paper; markers; pencils; dowel rods, or paper tubes; clear tape or glue; yarn or ribbon
	Saying Good-bye	• *Weekly Bible Reader®* Issue 10	• none

Focus In (15 minutes)

Life Focus
❤ We can know and understand God's Word.

Step 1 • Use one of these activities to help children **explore things they know and understand.** Use the Bible Memory activity to introduce the memory verses.

Welcome
- Welcome each child by name.
- Do check-in procedures you follow (name and security tags, offering, attendance chart, etc.).
- Early arrivers will enjoy doing one or more of the activities described on page 58.

≡ *Quick Step* What Do You Know?

Let's think about things you know and understand. Distribute the cards to individual children, pairs, or small groups of children. Have each individual (or group) tell what she knows and understands about the object pictured on her card.

The following are a few things kids could mention about a few of the objects. Sun: is a star, the earth and other planets revolve around it, gives us light and warmth, crops need it to grow. Water: colorless liquid that falls as rain, can be frozen, need it in order to live. Rainbow: seen in the sky, an arc of seven different colors, caused by the bending of sunlight as it shines through water vapor.
- **What are some other things you know and understand?**
- **Who are some people that have helped you and continue to help you know about these and other things?** (parents, family, friends, teachers)

There are lots of things we can know and understand. We're going to learn that ❤ **we can know and understand God's Word.**

Materials
Resources Sheet 7 picture cards for Lesson 10

DISCUSS

Option   If You Know

Let's think about things you know and understand. When I say something that you know and understand, raise both hands and say "I know."

Apples can be red, green, or yellow. (I know) **Clouds can be white and green. Cats come in lots of different colors.** (I know) **Water falls from the moon. 2+2=4.** (I know) **Milk comes from kangaroos. Most people have two eyes.** (I know) **The Bible is God's Word.** (I know) **Rainbows happen after tornadoes. Elevators go up and down.** (I know) **Exercise is good for our bodies.** (I know) **Eating candy is healthier than eating broccoli. Birds fly using their wings.** (I know)
- **What are some other things you know and understand?**
- **Who are some people that have helped you and continue to help you know about these and other things?** (parents, family, friends, teachers)

There are lots of things we can know and understand. We're going to learn that ❤ **we can know and understand God's Word.**

Materials
none

Action

Added Fun!
Let kids name things while the rest of the class says if it's something they know or not.

Bible Memory   Acts 4:19, 20

From the Bible, read aloud Acts 4:19, 20 but leave out the words "But Peter and John replied." **These verses are our Bible Memory verses. Do you remember who said these words?** (Peter and John) **Peter and John couldn't help but tell others about Jesus.** Play "Judge for Yourselves" and invite kids to join in. Words can be found in a printable file on the CD. **Peter and John could tell others about Jesus because they knew and understood God's Word. Did you know that ❤ we can know and understand God's Word too? We can!**

Materials
Bible, *Resources* CD Track 11 and the "Judge for Yourselves" Posters and Activities printable file (*NIV* or *KJV*), CD player

DISCUSS

Transition to Explore His Word
See the *Resources* CD Transition Tips printable file. As children gather, make sure you have all the materials you need.

Life Focus
❤ We can know and understand God's Word.

Explore His Word (20 minutes)

Step 2 • Use all of these activities to help children **tell how Philip helped the man from Ethiopia understand God's Word** and develop Bible skills.

Bible Background for the Teacher

The man from Ethiopia was a eunuch. Being a eunuch could mean he had had an operation that made it impossible for him to have children, or sometimes *eunuch* was a title for someone holding a high governmental office. This non-Jewish man was either a proselyte or near-proselyte to Judaism since we know he worshiped God and had a copy of the Scriptures. Candace was a title for the queen mother of Ethiopia, much like Pharaoh was used as a title for the rulers in Egypt.

God directly intervened to arrange the meeting between Philip and the official. An angel, the Holy Spirit, and Philip's obedience worked to bring about the meeting between the two men.

Since it was customary practice to read aloud, it was not unusual that Philip heard the man reading the Scriptures. Whether the man already understood about water baptism, or it was in response to Philip's appeal to follow Jesus, the official proclaimed his commitment to Jesus when he was baptized. It is believed that this man helped spread the gospel message into Africa.

Acts 8:39 is a very unusual expression of God's power. Although we have no further explanation as to *how* the Spirit moved Philip, we do see a similar phenomenon with the disciples and their boat in John 6:15-21.

Worship Time
If you want to offer a time of worship, see the *Resources* CD Worship Time Ideas printable file for suggestions.

Materials
white board, dry-erase marker, Bibles, *Resources* Sheet 7 pictures 10a and 10b, coins, paper lunch bag, *Teaching Picture* 10

Bible Story

Before Class
Put some coins in the paper lunch bag.

Story Option
Play the recorded Bible story from the *Resources* CD Track 14.

Philip Teaches a Man from Ethiopia   (Acts 8:26-40)

Write "Matthew, Mark, Luke, John, Acts" on the board and say the names aloud. **Which section of the Bible starts with these five books?** (New Testament) **These books tell about Jesus and His church. The Bible story once again comes from the New Testament book of Acts.** Write "Acts 8:26" on the board after "John." Help children find Acts in the table of contents and then help them turn to Acts 8:26. Ask for a volunteer to read the verse.

You all need to be involved in today's Bible story. When you hear an official ask a question, use your index finger to draw a question mark in the air. Have the kids practice this. **And you need to listen for how Philip helped the official understand God's Word.**

(Have your Bible open to Acts 8.) The road was long and dusty *(show 10a)*. The man must have wondered how much farther he had to go on his long journey back to his home in the country of Ethiopia. The man had gone to Jerusalem to worship and was now returning to his country and his job. He was an important person. He was the queen's treasurer which meant he took care of all the money. *(Remove some coins from the bag to show the kids.)* As he rode along in his chariot, the Ethiopian official began to read in his Bible-scroll from the book of Isaiah. *(Point out the scroll and chariot in the picture.)*

About that time, an angel of the Lord spoke to Philip, a follower of Jesus. The angel said, "Go to the road that leads down to Gaza from Jerusalem—the desert road." Philip went.

On the desert road, Philip saw the official from Ethiopia riding in a chariot. The Holy Spirit told Philip to go to the man's chariot. Philip not only went to the chariot, he ran toward it. Philip heard the man reading the book of Isaiah from the Scriptures.

Philip asked the official if he understood what he was reading. The official said, "How can I understand it? *(Kids draw question mark.)* I need someone to explain it to me."

(Show Teaching Picture 10.) The official asked Philip to ride with him in the chariot. Together they read from the book of Isaiah. The official was reading

Explore His Word (continued)

a Scripture that described Jesus. Philip told the man all the wonderful things Jesus had done. Philip told the good news of Jesus.

While they were traveling, the official said, "Look, here is water. Why shouldn't I be baptized?" *(Kids draw question mark; v. 37).*

(Show 10b.) Philip was glad to baptize the official. Philip and the official both went down into the water, and Philip baptized him. The Ethiopian official then went back to his country very excited and happy that someone had told him about Jesus. Philip was probably very happy also. Then the Holy Spirit took Philip away to preach the good news about Jesus in other places.

Bible Review Activity

How did Philip help the official from Ethiopia understand God's Word? (Philip read the Scriptures with the man. Philip told the man all the wonderful things Jesus had done—including how Jesus died and came back to life.) **Let's see what else you remember.** Distribute the activity pages and stickers. Read the directions aloud and do the page together.

As time permits, play a review game. Have kids sit in a circle. They are to pass the bag of coins around the circle until you say "Philip told about Jesus!" The child holding the bag of coins will answer a question. Make sure everyone gets to answer at least one question. For more questions about the story, see the Review Questions on the CD.

• **What was the official reading?** (the book of Isaiah from a Bible-scroll)
• **Who told Philip to go to the desert road?** (an angel of the Lord)
• **Who told Philip to go to the official's chariot?** (the Holy Spirit)
• **When the official saw some water, what did he want to do?** (be baptized)

Philip helped the official know and understand God's Word. We're going to learn that ❤ we can know and understand God's Word too.

Bible Skill Builder and Bible Memory Activity

Write "John, Mark, Acts, Matthew, Luke" on the board. **Did I write these Bible book names in the right order?** (no) **Who can tell us the correct order?** (Matthew, Mark, Luke, John, Acts) Rewrite the names in the right order. **These five books are the first books of the Old Testament. Is that right?** (no) **What are they?** (first five books of the New Testament) **The first four books tell us about Jesus. The book of Acts tells us about the early years of Jesus' church.** Write "Acts 4:19, 20" on the board. **Let's find our Bible Memory verses.** Help the children turn to Acts 4:19, 20. Ask for volunteers to read the verses.

Display the Bible Memory poster. Point to the words as you lead the kids in reading the verses together. Rearrange the order of the verses. Ask kids to put the poster back in the right order. Do this several times. Then ask everyone to join in reading the Bible Memory verses together. **Peter and John were able to tell others about Jesus because they knew and understood God's Word. It's important that ❤ we know and understand God's Word so we can tell others about Jesus too!**

Expert Tip

"Today's children require and expect variety, activity, visuals, and plenty of application to their current lives."
—*Steve Alley*

Materials
Activities p. 27 and corresponding stickers, coins in a paper lunch bag, *Resources* CD Review Questions printable file

Added Fun!
Give each child a coin to serve as a reminder of today's Bible story.

Materials
white board, dry-erase marker, Bibles, *Resources* Sheet 6 Bible Memory poster, reusable adhesive

Life Focus
❤ We can know and understand God's Word.

Make It Real (15 minutes)

Step 3 • Use one of these activities to help children **discover what or who can help them understand God's Word.**

Materials
Activities p. 28, colored pencils or markers

Activity Page

☰ *Quick Step* Who or What Can Help?

We've learned how Philip helped the official know and understand God's Word. Let's discover what or who can help you understand God's Word. Distribute the activity pages and colored pencils or markers. Read the directions aloud and do the page together.

• **Can parents help you understand God's Word?** (yes) Kids should draw a line from that picture to the Bible. **How?** (They can read God's Word to me. They can tell me about Jesus.)

• **Can a cat help you understand God's Word?** (no)

• **Can prayer help you understand God's Word?** (yes) **How?** (I can pray and ask God to help me understand it.)

Do the same with all the pictures.

There are lots of people and things that can help us so that ❤ we can know and understand God's Word. We want to understand God's Word so we will be able to share it with others and tell people about Jesus.

Materials
paper, pencil, white board, dry-erase markers and eraser

Game

Option Drawing Game

We've learned how Philip helped the official know and understand God's Word. Let's discover what or who can help you understand God's Word. Before class, write the following on separate slips of paper: parents, grandparents, prayer, book of Bible stories, friends, preachers, and Sunday school teachers.

Divide the kids into two teams. Tell kids that they are going to draw some people and objects that can help them understand God's Word. Have a child from one team choose a slip of paper and draw a picture of that person or object on the board. As the child draws, the kids on her team can call out guesses of what is being drawn. If they don't guess correctly, the other team can make a guess. Award points as desired. After each picture, discuss how that person or object can help them better understand God's Word.

There are lots of people and things that can help us so that ❤ we can know and understand God's Word. We want to understand God's Word so we will be able to share it with others and tell people about Jesus.

Materials
Weekly Bible Reader® Issue 10

LISTEN

Option Story from *Weekly Bible Reader®*

We've learned how Philip helped the official know and understand God's Word. Let's discover what or who can help you understand God's Word. Read "Telling a Friend."

• **Who or what can help you understand God's Word?** (See the activities above for possible responses.)

❤ We can know and understand God's Word, and there are lots of people and things that can help us.

Live It Out (10 minutes)

Step 4 • Use one of these activities to help children **plan ways to better understand God's Word.**

≡ *Quick Step* What We Can Do

We've learned that there are lots of people and things that can help us so that ❤ **we can know and understand God's Word. Now you need to plan ways you can better understand God's Word.** If you did not display the title card "Here Is What We Can Do!" and Lessons 7–9 cards on a bulletin board or wall in the previous lessons, you can do so now. Then attach the Lesson 10 card on the board or wall. Read the text aloud on all the cards.

Before class, label half-sheets of paper with these titles: parents, prayer, Sunday school teachers, preachers, friends, books of Bible stories, and grand-parents. If desired, draw a large outline of a Bible on each paper.

Show kids the papers. **On these papers are the names of people or things that can help you understand God's Word. I would like for you to sign your name on those papers that tell the people or things that you plan on using to better understand the Bible.** Show kids the paper with "parents" on it. **If you plan on asking your parents to help you better understand God's Word, come and sign your name on this paper.** Give time for kids to do so. Do the same with all the papers. Then attach the papers on the board or wall under the Lesson 10 card.

Close with a time of prayer. Pray and ask God to help the children better understand His Word.

Materials
Resources Sheet 8 "Here Is What We Can Do!" title card and cards for Lessons 7–10, pushpins or reusable adhesive, construction paper, markers

Option Scroll Reminders

We've learned that there are lots of people and things that can help us so that ❤ **we can know and understand God's Word. Now you need to plan ways you can better understand God's Word.** Tell kids that they are going to make scrolls to remind them that they should keep learning about God's Word so they can better understand it. Distribute paper and markers. Kids should write or draw pictures of people and things they plan on using to help them better understand God's Word. When kids are done, give them the rest of the supplies. Help kids put the ends of the papers around the pencils, dowel rods, or paper tubes and help them attach the ends with tape or glue. Kids can use yarn or ribbons to tie the ends of their scrolls together.

Have kids bring their completed scrolls to a closing time of prayer. Have each child share what she wrote or drew on her scroll. Invite children to pray for God's help to better understand His Word.

Materials
paper; markers; pencils, dowel rods, or paper tubes; clear tape or glue
(optional: yarn or ribbon)

Saying Good-bye
• Distribute Issue 10 of *Weekly Bible Reader*®.
• Make sure children have projects and activity sheets they have done.
• If you have time before parents arrive, use some of the activities on page 58.
• Remind parents that a weekly *Faith & Family* page is available online to print and use with their child at home. See www.heartshaper.com.

Evaluate
• How well do the children understand the importance of better understanding God's Word?
• In what ways did you help the children better understand God's Word?

Peter and Tabitha

Bible Focus: Acts 9:36-42
Bible Memory: But Peter and John replied, "Which is right in God's eyes: to listen to you, or to him? You be the judges! As for us, we cannot help speaking about what we have seen and heard" (Acts 4:19, 20).
Life Focus: ❤ We can believe in Jesus.

Heart to Heart

It's sometimes hard to know truth from fiction, isn't it? Maybe you've received e-mails or heard of strange stories that people claim are true and you believed them. However, you later learned that they are nothing but urban legends.

You can believe in Jesus. And you can believe what God's Word says about Jesus. But don't believe everything you hear about Jesus without making sure that it lines up with what's in the Bible. Continue to be a student of the Bible, learning all that you can, so that you can better help the children in your class believe in Jesus too.

Lesson 11 at a Glance

Step	Quick Step	HeartShaper Materials	Other Materials
Step 1 **Focus In** Use one of these activities to help children *identify things they believe.*	*Quick Step* What Do You Believe? **Option** Will It Fall? **Bible Memory** *Use this activity to introduce the Bible Memory verses.*	• reproducible p. 96 • none • *Resources* Sheet 6 Bible Memory poster	• pencils or markers • items kids can drop (see the activity) • Bible, reusable adhesive
Step 2 **Explore His Word** Use all of these activities to help children *tell what Peter did that helped people believe in Jesus* and develop Bible skills.	Peter and Tabitha Bible Review Activity Bible Skill Builder and Bible Memory Activity	• *Resources* Sheet 6 Peter headpiece, Sheet 8 Tabitha and friends of Tabitha name cards and picture 11a, CD including the "Judge for Yourselves" and Review Questions printable files; *Teaching Picture* 11	• white board, dry-erase marker, Bibles, hole punch, yarn, CD player
Step 3 **Make It Real** Use one of these activities to help children *discover things to believe about Jesus.*	*Quick Step* What I Believe **Option** Stand Up If You Believe **Option** Story from *Weekly Bible Reader®*	• *Activities* p. 29 • none • *Weekly Bible Reader®* Issue 11	• scissors, construction paper, glue, markers • none • none
Step 4 **Live It Out** Use one of these activities to help children *name what they believe about Jesus.*	*Quick Step* What I Believe Posters **Option** What We Can Do Saying Good-bye	• none • *Resources* Sheet 8 title card and cards for Lessons 7–11 • *Weekly Bible Reader®* Issue 11	• posters made in the Step 3 *Quick Step* activity • pushpins or reusable adhesive, construction paper, markers • none

Focus In (15 minutes)

Step 1 • Use one of these activities to help children **identify things they believe.**

Welcome
- Welcome each child by name.
- Do check-in procedures you follow (name and security tags, offering, attendance chart, etc.).
- Early arrivers will enjoy doing one or more of the activities described on page 58.

≡ *Quick Step* What Do You Believe?

Let's think about things we believe. Before class, make copies of the reproducible page. Distribute the pages and pencils or markers. Read the directions aloud and do the page together. Ask for volunteers to read each sentence aloud. After each sentence, tell kids to circle the sentence if it's something they believe is true. After kids have circled or not circled a sentence, ask:

• **Do you believe that? If you do, raise your hand.** Do the same for all the sentences.

Ask kids to turn their papers over. Assign each child to draw what he believes is true about a certain thing or person. Examples: Ask children to draw what they believe is true about dogs, the sun, the sky, cats, grass, rain, the earth, and so forth. When children are finished, let them share what they drew.

• **What are some other things you believe are true?** (Leaves grow on trees. My parents love me. Jesus loves me. God made everything.)

There are a lot of things that we can believe are true. We're going to learn that ❤ we can believe in Jesus.

Materials
reproducible p. 96, pencils or markers

Activity Page

Option   Will It Fall?

Have you ever thought about all the things that you believe are true? Let's explore a few things you believe by doing some experiments. Have a child choose one of the items and hold it. Ask him to tell what he believes would happen if he were to drop the item. Then have him drop the item. Let other children have a turn and do the same for all the items.

• **What do you believe will happen to any item that you drop?** (It will fall to the ground.)

• **What are some other things you believe are true?** (Leaves grow on trees. My parents love me. Jesus loves me. God made everything.)

• **Why do you believe those things are true?** (Just know it's true. Have seen it happen. It always happens.)

There are a lot of things that we can believe are true. We're going to learn that ❤ we can believe in Jesus.

Materials
items kids can drop (leaf, feather, coin, paper, pencil, beanbag)

Discover

Bible Memory   Acts 4:19, 20

Read aloud Acts 4:19, 20 from the Bible. **Let's say our Bible Memory verses together.** Display the Bible Memory poster and lead the kids in reading the verses. Remove one of the strips of the poster and lead kids in saying the verses again. Remove another strip and lead kids in saying the verses again. Keep removing the strips until they have all been removed. Then see how many kids can say the verses from memory. **Peter and John told others about Jesus because they believed in Him. We can tell others about Jesus because ❤ we can believe in Jesus too!**

Materials
Bible, *Resources* Sheet 6 Bible Memory poster, reusable adhesive

Transition to Explore His Word
See the *Resources* CD Transition Tips printable file. As children gather, make sure you have all the materials you need.

Life Focus
❤ We can believe in Jesus.

Explore His Word (20 minutes)

Step 2 • Use all of these activities to help children **tell what Peter did that helped people believe in Jesus** and develop Bible skills.

Bible Background for the Teacher
Joppa was about 38 miles from Jerusalem and served as its seaport. The town of Lydda was about 12 miles from Joppa. The woman's name in Hebrew was Tabitha and in Greek, Dorcas. Tabitha was a woman who served others. She was kind and was known for her good works on behalf of others, especially poor people and widows.

We are not told why the friends of Tabitha wanted Peter to come. Maybe they wanted consolation. But more likely they wanted Peter to restore Tabitha to life. They no doubt knew that Peter had been involved in many miraculous healings, although he had never raised anyone to life.

Peter had been present when Jesus raised to life Jairus's daughter, the widow's son, and Lazarus. Peter now calls upon the power of God to raise Tabitha. The great result of this miracle was that many people believed in the Lord. Miraculous healings in Scripture often served the purpose of showing God's power and authenticating His Word in order to help people believe (John 20:30, 31).

Worship Time
If you want to offer a time of worship, see the *Resources* CD Worship Time Ideas printable file for suggestions.

Materials
white board; dry-erase marker; Bibles; *Resources* Sheet 6 Peter's headpiece, Sheet 8 Tabitha and friends of Tabitha name cards and picture 11a; *Teaching Picture* 11; hole punch; yarn

Before Class
Punch two holes in the "Tabitha" name card and two holes in the "friends of Tabitha" name card; string both with yarn.

Peter and Tabitha   (Acts 9:36-42)
What are the names of the first four books of the New Testament? (Matthew, Mark, Luke, John) Lead the children in saying the names together. **Who do these four books mainly tell about?** (Jesus) **What book comes after John?** (Acts) Write "Acts 9:36" on the board. **How can we find the book of Acts in our Bibles?** (Look in the table of contents, look in the New Testament section, find Acts, and turn to it.) Help children turn to Acts 9:36 and ask for a volunteer to read the verse.

Choose a child to wear the Peter headpiece and act out what Peter did. Choose a child to wear the "Tabitha" name card and a child to wear the "friends of Tabitha" name card and act out what they did.

You all need to be involved in today's Bible story. When you hear me say the woman's name, Tabitha, you need to say "who did good things." Have the kids practice this. **And you need to listen for what Peter did that helped people believe in Jesus.**

(Have your Bible open to Acts 9.) There were followers of Jesus in many cities. These were men and women who believed in Jesus and followed Him. **Tabitha** *(kids say "who did good things")* was a follower of Jesus who lived in the city of Joppa. **Tabitha** helped people who were poor and women who were widows. She made clothes for people, and she was always doing good things.

One day **Tabitha** became sick and died. Some friends put her in an upstairs room and then sent two men to find Peter. The two men found Peter in the nearby town of Lydda. The men said to Peter, "Please come with us." Peter went with the men to the town of Joppa.

When Peter got to the house, he went to the upstairs room where **Tabitha** was. Many women were there, and they were crying. They showed Peter some of the clothes she had made *(show 11a)*. They were sad that their friend **Tabitha** had died.

Peter sent everyone out of the room. He got on his knees and prayed to God. Peter then looked at **Tabitha** and said, "Get up, **Tabitha**!"

Tabitha opened her eyes and sat up. *(Show Teaching Picture 11.)* Peter took her by the hand and helped her stand up. Peter told all the people to come into the room. He wanted to show them that **Tabitha** was alive! They must have been so happy to see their friend alive again.

People in the city of Joppa heard that Jesus' power had brought **Tabitha** back to life. Because of this, many people believed in the Lord.

Bible Review Activity

What did Peter do that helped people believe in Jesus? (By the power of Jesus, he raised Tabitha from the dead.) **Let's see what else you remember.** Have the children sit in a circle and pass the Peter headpiece until you say "Believe in Jesus!" The child holding the headpiece can wear it while answering a review question. For more questions about the story, see the Review Questions on the CD.

- **In what city did Tabitha live?** (Joppa)
- **Whom did Tabitha help?** (people who were poor and women who were widows)
- **How did Tabitha help people?** (She made clothes for people, and she was always doing good things.)
- **Who was sent to get Peter after Tabitha died?** (two men)
- **What did Tabitha's friends show Peter?** (some of the clothes she had made)
- **Whom did Peter send out of Tabitha's room?** (everyone)
- **What did Peter say to Tabitha?** (Get up.)
- **What had brought Tabitha back to life?** (Jesus' power)

The people in Joppa believed in Jesus because they knew that Jesus' power had raised Tabitha to life. ❤ **We can believe in Jesus too!**

Materials
Resources Sheet 6
Peter's headpiece,
CD Review Questions
printable file

Bible Skill Builder and Bible Memory Activity

Look in the table of contents in your Bibles. Would you look in the Old Testament or New Testament to find the books that tell about Jesus? (New) **Which four books of the New Testament tell about Jesus?** (Matthew, Mark, Luke, John) **Which book of the New Testament tells about the early years of Jesus' church?** (Acts) **Let's find our Bible Memory verses, Acts 4:19, 20.** Help the children turn to Acts 4:19, 20. Ask the children to read or say the verses together. Also encourage the children to say the verses by themselves.

Before class, make copies of the words for "Judge for Yourselves." Distribute copies of the words. Go over the suggested motions, play "Judge for Yourselves," and invite kids to join in. **Peter and John weren't afraid to speak boldly about Jesus because they believed in Jesus. Remember that we shouldn't be afraid to speak boldly about Jesus because** ❤ **we can believe in Jesus too!**

Materials
Bibles, *Resources* CD
Track 11 including the
"Judge for Yourselves" Posters and
Activities printable file (*NIV* or *KJV*),
CD player

Expert Tip
"In order for discipline to be effective, the consequence must be related to the deed as much as possible."
—*Jody Capehart*

Life Focus
❤ We can believe in Jesus.

Make It Real (15 minutes)

Step 3 • Use one of these activities to help children **discover things to believe about Jesus.**

Materials
Activities p. 29, scissors, construction paper, glue, markers

Activity Page

☰ *Quick Step* What I Believe Posters

We've learned that Peter helped the people believe in Jesus when Peter raised Tabitha from the dead by the power of Jesus. Let's discover things to believe about Jesus. Distribute the activity pages and scissors. Read the directions aloud. Have kids cut out the title and sentences.

Some of these sentences tell things that the Bible says are true and that we can believe about Jesus. But some of these sentences tell things that we don't learn about Jesus from the Bible. Ask for volunteers to read each sentence. Decide together which sentences can be believed because the Bible tells us. The other sentences should be set aside. (Not in the Bible: Jesus made a lot of money. Jesus was short and climbed a tree. Jesus traveled by car.)

Distribute construction paper, glue, and markers. Have kids glue the title and sentences to construction paper to make posters about Jesus. Kids could also decorate their posters with markers.

• **What are some other things you believe about Jesus?** (He healed people. He stopped a storm. He is powerful. Wise men worshiped Him. He cares about all people.)

Jesus is special! He does things no one else can do. ❤ We can believe in Jesus!

Materials
none

Action

Option   Stand Up If You Believe

We've learned that Peter helped the people believe in Jesus when Peter raised Tabitha from the dead by the power of Jesus. Let's discover things to believe about Jesus. Tell the children that you will read some sentences. They are to stand up and say "I believe!" if the sentence tells something about Jesus they learned from the Bible and believe. Have children sit down after each sentence.

Jesus is God's Son. (Kids stand up and say "I believe!") **Jesus is powerful.** (stand up) **Jesus worked at a factory. Jesus loves us.** (stand up) **Jesus did miracles.** (stand up) **Jesus wore running shoes. Jesus died on the cross.** (stand up) **Jesus was born in Bethlehem.** (stand up) **Jesus traveled by airplane. Jesus walked on water.** (stand up) **Jesus stopped a storm.** (stand up) **Jesus cares about all people.** (stand up)

Jesus is special! He does things no one else can do. ❤ We can believe in Jesus!

Materials
Weekly Bible Reader®
Issue 11

LISTEN

Option   Story from *Weekly Bible Reader*®

We've learned that Peter helped the people believe in Jesus when he raised Tabitha from the dead by the power of Jesus. Let's discover things to believe about Jesus. Read "I Believe."

• **What are things we can believe about Jesus?** (See the activities above for possible responses.)

Jesus is special! He does things no one else can do. ❤ We can believe in Jesus!

Life Focus
❤ We can believe in Jesus.

Step 4 • Use one of these activities to help children **name what they believe about Jesus.**

≡ Quick Step   What I Believe Posters

❤ **We can believe in Jesus! Now it's time for you to name what you believe about Jesus.** Have children look at the posters they made in the Step 3 *Quick Step.* If you did not have kids make the posters in Step 3, they could make them now. Ask each child to name at least one thing on the poster or something not on the poster that they believe about Jesus. Tell kids to put their posters where they will see them often and be reminded of just how great Jesus is and all the things they believe about Him.

Close with a time of prayer. Tell kids that you will pray sentence prayers that name things we can believe about Jesus. If they agree with what you pray, they should repeat the prayers. **Dear God** (pause; kids repeat), **I believe that Jesus is powerful.** (pause) **I believe that Jesus is Your Son.** (pause) **I believe that Jesus did miracles.** (pause) **I believe that Jesus cares about everyone.** (pause) **I believe that Jesus died on the cross.** (pause) **I believe that Jesus rose from the dead.** (pause) **I believe that Jesus loves me.** (pause) **In Jesus' name, amen.**

Materials
posters made in the Step 3 *Quick Step* activity (*Activities* p. 29)

Option   What We Can Do

❤ **We can believe in Jesus! Now it's time for you to name what you believe about Jesus.** If you did not display the title card "Here Is What We Can Do!" and Lessons 7–10 cards on a bulletin board or wall in the previous lessons, you can do so now. Then attach the Lesson 11 card on the board or wall. Read the text aloud on all the cards.

Give kids construction paper and markers. Ask them to draw a picture of at least one thing they believe about Jesus. When they are done, they can attach their drawings to the board or wall under the Lesson 11 card. Let all kids share what they drew.

Have kids gather for a time of prayer. Encourage all children to pray silently. Then close by praying, **Thank You, God, that we can believe in Jesus. In His name we pray, amen.**

Materials
Resources Sheet 8 "Here Is What We Can Do!" title card and cards for Lessons 7–11, pushpins or reusable adhesive, construction paper, markers

Saying Good-bye

• Distribute Issue 11 of *Weekly Bible Reader®* and the *Activities* page 31 Unit 2 Bible Memory poster and stickers if you have not already done so. Also distribute the *Activities* Mystery Ink™ pages if you have not already done so.

• Make sure children have projects and activity sheets they have done.

• If you have time before parents arrive, use some of the activities on page 58.

• Remind parents that a weekly *Faith & Family* page is available online to print and use with their child at home. See www.heartshaper.com.

Evaluate
• In what ways did the children show they believe in Jesus?
• Take some extra time to evaluate. What things will you continue doing? What things will you change to better meet the needs of the children in your class?

Tape or glue a
jumbo craft stick here.

Copy on green card stock and cut out.
Or trace shape onto green construction
paper and cut out.

Art by Kathryn Marlin

Use with Triumphal Entry lesson.

Early Elementary Teacher, HeartShaper® Curriculum
Permission is granted to reproduce this page for ministry purposes only—not for resale.

89

Jesus was buried in a tomb.

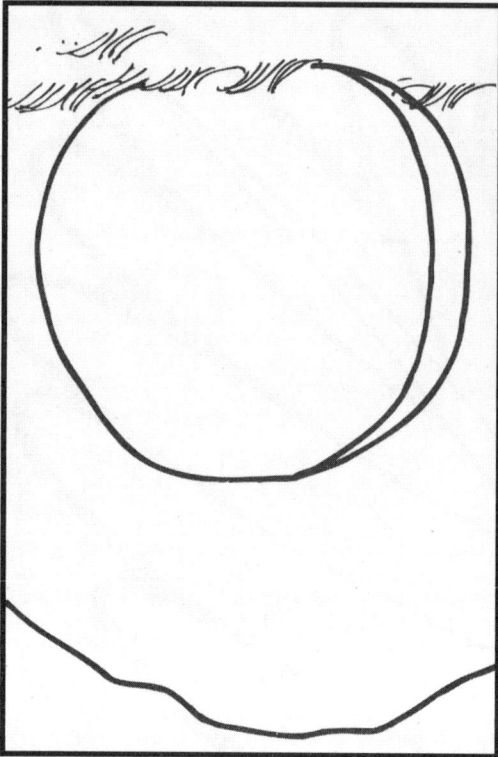

Jesus died on the cross.

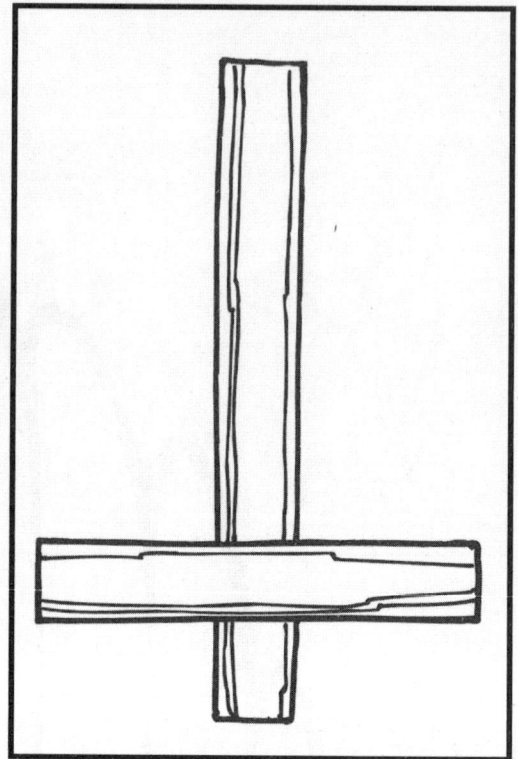

Jesus came back to life.
Jesus is alive!

Jesus is alive!

Art by Len Ebert

Use with Jesus' Resurrection lesson.

Early Elementary Teacher, HeartShaper® Curriculum

Jesus can do miracles!

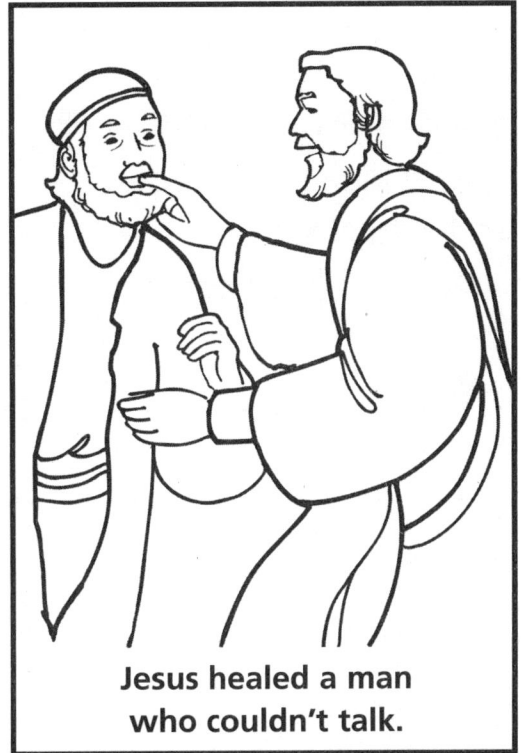

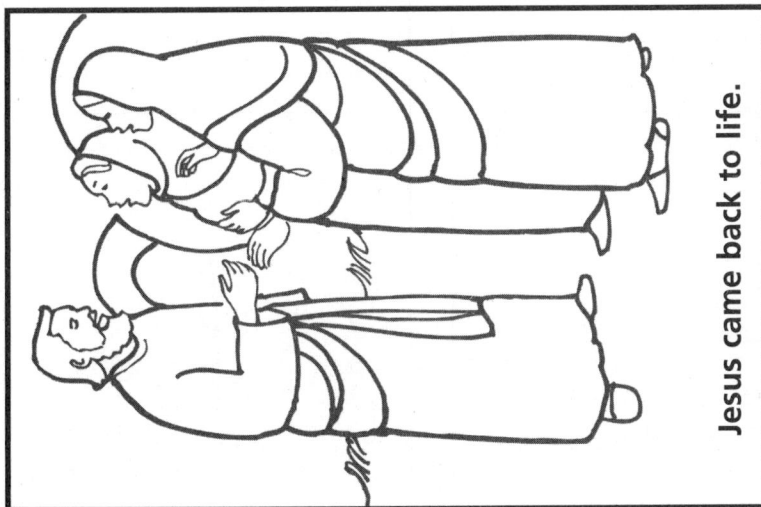

Jesus healed a man who couldn't talk.

Pick up your mat and walk.

Jesus healed a man at a pool.

Jesus came back to life.

Jesus calmed a storm.

Art by Len Ebert

Use with Lesson 2.

Early Elementary Teacher, HeartShaper® Curriculum
Permission is granted to reproduce this page for ministry purposes only—not for resale.

91

Use the Word Bank and pictures to answer the riddles.

Move your arms,
And kick real hard.
Do this fast
And you'll go far!

You can _____ .

Word Bank
☆ boat
☆ swim
☆ water
☆ waves

Up and down I go,
As far as eye can see.
When the wind blows,
I'm big as big can be.

I am _____ .

Sit in me
I'll keep you dry,
As we float
Beneath the sky.

I am a

_____ .

If you want to stand,
Do a little thinking.
Don't stand on me or
You'll do a little sinking.

I am _____ .

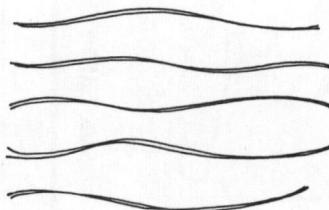

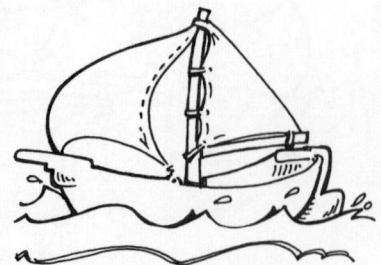

Art by Corbin Hillam

Use with Lesson 4.

STOP

YIELD

GO

ONE WAY

Use with Lessons 4 and 6.

What's Great?

In each row, circle what you think is great.

1.

2.

3.

4.

5.

6.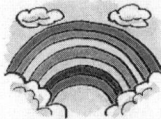

7.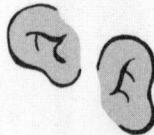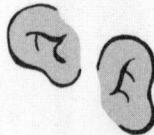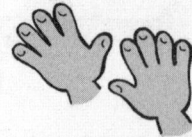

8.

Art by Michael Streff

Use with Lesson 6.

Early Elementary Teacher, HeartShaper® Curriculum

Jesus is the Son of God.

Jesus loves everyone.

Art by Ron Wheeler

Use with Lesson 8.

What Do You Believe?

Circle the sentences that you believe are true.

1. I believe that can be pink.

2. I believe that can fly.

3. I believe that can talk.

4. I believe that are good.

5. I believe that the is flat.

6. I believe that an is good.

7. I believe that the is in the sky.

8. I believe that a can fly.

Art by Michael Streff

Use with Lesson 11.

Early Elementary Teacher, HeartShaper® Curriculum